CHAPTER I.—SENTENCES.

A *Sentence* is an assemblage of words, making complete sense, and always containing a nominative and a verb; as, "Reward sweetens labour."

The *principal parts* of a sentence are usually three; namely, the SUBJECT, or nominative,—the attribute, or finite VERB,—and the case put after, or the OBJECT[322] governed by the verb: as, "*Crimes deserve punishment.*"

The *other* or *subordinate parts* depend upon these, either as primary or as secondary *adjuncts*; as, "*High* crimes *justly* deserve *very severe* punishments."

Sentences are usually said to be of two kinds, *simple* and *compound*. [323]

A *simple sentence* is a sentence which consists of one single assertion, supposition, command, question, or exclamation; as, "David and Jonathan loved each other."—"If thine enemy hunger."—"Do violence to no man."—"Am I not an apostle?"—*1 Cor.*, ix, 1. "What immortal glory shall I have acquired!"—HOOKE: *Mur. Seq.*, p. 71.

A *compound sentence* is a sentence which consists of two or more simple ones either expressly or tacitly connected; as, "Send men to Joppa, *and* call for Simon, *whose* surname is Peter; *who* shall tell thee words, *whereby* thou and all thy house shall be saved."—*Acts*, xi, 13. "The more the works of Cowper are read, the more his readers will find reason to admire the variety and the extent, the graces and the energy, of his literary talents."—HAYLEY: *Mur. Seq.*, p. 250.

A *clause*, or *member*, is a subdivision of a compound sentence; and is itself a sentence, either simple or compound: as, "If thine enemy be hungry, give him bread to eat; if he be thirsty, give him water to drink."—*Prov.*, xxv, 21.[324]

A *phrase* is two or more words which express some relation of different ideas, but no entire proposition; as, "By the means appointed."—"To be plain with you."—"Having loved his own."

Words that are omitted by *ellipsis*, and that are necessarily understood in order to complete the construction, (and only such,) must be supplied in parsing.

The *leading principles* to be observed in the construction of sentences, are embraced in the following twenty-four rules, which are arranged, as nearly as possible, in the order of the parts of speech.

THE RULES OF SYNTAX.

RULE I.—ARTICLES.

Articles relate to the nouns which they limit.

RULE II.—NOMINATIVES.

A Noun or a Pronoun which is the subject of a finite verb, must be in the nominative case.

RULE III.—APPOSITION. A Noun or a personal Pronoun used to explain a preceding noun or pronoun, is put, by apposition, in the same case.

RULE IV.—POSSESSIVES.

A Noun or a Pronoun in the possessive case, is governed by the name of the thing possessed.

RULE V.—OBJECTIVES.

A Noun or a Pronoun made the object of an active-transitive verb or participle, is governed by it in the objective case.

RULE VI.—SAME CASES.

A Noun or a Pronoun put after a verb or participle not transitive, agrees in case with a preceding noun or pronoun referring to the same thing.

RULE VII.—OBJECTIVES.

A Noun or a Pronoun made the object of a preposition, is governed by it in the objective case.

RULE VIII.—NOM. ABSOLUTE.

A Noun or a Pronoun is put absolute in the nominative, when its case depends on no other word.

RULE IX.—ADJECTIVES.

Adjectives relate to nouns or pronouns.

RULE X.—PRONOUNS.

A Pronoun must agree with its antecedent, or the noun or pronoun which it represents, in person, number, and gender.

RULE XI—PRONOUNS.

When the antecedent is a collective noun conveying the idea of plurality, the Pronoun must agree with it in the plural number.

RULE XII.—PRONOUNS.

When a Pronoun has two or more antecedents connected by *and*, it must agree with them jointly in the plural, because they are taken together.

RULE XIII.—PRONOUNS.

When a Pronoun has two or more antecedents connected by *or* or *nor*, it must agree with them singly, and not as if taken together.

RULE XIV.—FINITE VERBS.

Every finite Verb must agree with its subject, or nominative, in person and number.

RULE XV.—FINITE VERBS.

When the nominative is a collective noun conveying the idea of plurality, the Verb must agree with it in the plural number.

RULE XVI.—FINITE VERBS.

When a Verb has two or more nominatives connected by *and*, it must agree with them jointly in the plural, because they are taken together.

RULE XVII.—FINITE VERBS.

When a Verb has two or more nominatives connected by *or* or *nor*, it must agree with them singly, and not as if taken together.

RULE XVIII.—INFINITIVES.

The Infinitive Mood is governed in general by the preposition TO, which commonly connects it to a finite verb.

RULE XIX.—INFINITIVES.

The active verbs, *bid, dare, feel, hear, let, make, need, see,* and their participles, usually take the Infinitive after them without the preposition TO.

RULE XX.—PARTICIPLES.

Participles relate to nouns or pronouns, or else are governed by prepositions.

RULE XXI.—ADVERBS.

Adverbs relate to verbs, participles, adjectives, or other adverbs.

RULE XXII.—CONJUNCTIONS.

Conjunctions connect words, sentences, or parts of sentences.

RULE XXIII.—PREPOSITIONS.

Prepositions show the relations of words, and of the things or thoughts expressed by them.

RULE XXIV.—INTERJECTIONS.

Interjections have no dependent construction; they are put absolute, either alone, or with other words.

GENERAL OR CRITICAL OBSERVATIONS ON SYNTAX.

OBS. 1.—An explanation of the relation, agreement, government, and arrangement, of words in sentences, constitutes that part of grammar which we call *Syntax*. But many grammarians, representing this branch of their subject as consisting of two parts only, "*concord* and *government*" say little or nothing of the *relation* and *arrangement* of words, except as these are involved in the others. The four things are essentially different in their nature, as may be seen by the definitions given above, yet not so distinct in practice that they can well be made the basis of any perfect division of the rules of syntax. I have therefore, on this occasion, preferred the order of the parts of speech; each of which will form a chapter in the Syntax of this work, as each forms a chapter in the Etymology.

OBS. 2.—*Agreement* and *concord* are one and the same thing. *Relation* and *agreement*, though different, may yet coincide, and be taken together. The latter is moreover naturally allied to the former. Seven of the ten parts of speech are, with a few exceptions, incapable of any agreement; of these the *relation* and *use* must be explained in parsing; and all *requisite agreement* between any of the rest, is confined to words that *relate* to each other. For one word may *relate* to an other and not *agree* with it; but there is never any *necessary agreement* between words that have not a *relation* one to the other, or a connexion according to the sense. Any similarity happening between unconnected words, is no syntactical concord, though it may rank the terms in the same class etymologically.

OBS. 3.—From these observations it may be seen, that the most important and most comprehensive principle of English syntax, is the simple *Relation* of words, according to the sense. To this head alone, ought to be referred all the rules of construction by which our articles, our nominatives, our adjectives, our participles, our adverbs, our conjunctions, our prepositions, and our interjections, are to be parsed. To the ordinary syntactical use of any of these, no rules of concord, government, or position, can at all apply. Yet so defective and erroneous are the schemes of syntax which are commonly found in our English grammars, that *no rules* of simple relation, none by which any of the above-named parts of speech can be consistently parsed, are in general to be found in them. If there are any exceptions to this censure, they are very few, and in treatises still marked with glaring defects in regard to the syntax of some of these parts of speech.

OBS. 4.—Grammarians, of course, do not utter falsehoods intentionally; but it is lamentable to see how often they pervert doctrine by untruths uttered ignorantly. It is the design of this pandect, to make every one who reads it, an intelligent judge of the *perversions*, as well as of the true doctrines, of English grammar. The following citations will show him the scope and parts which have commonly been assigned to our syntax: "The construction of sentences depends principally upon the *concord* or *agreement*, and the *regimen* or *government*, of words."—*Lowth's Gram.*, p. 68; *Churchill's*, 120. "Words in sentences have a *twofold relation* to one another; namely, that of *Concord* or Agreement; and that of *Government* or Influence."—*Dr. Adam's Latin and English Grammar*, p. 151. "The third part of Grammar is SYNTAX, which treats of the *agreement and construction* of words in a sentence."—*E. G. Greene's Grammatical Text-Book*, p. 15. "Syntax principally consists of two parts, *Concord* and *Government*."—*Murray's Gram.*, p. 142; *Ingersoll's*, 170; *Alger's*, 51; *R. C. Smith's*, 119; and many others. "Syntax consists of two parts, *Concord* and *Government*."—*Kirkham's Gram.*, p. 175; *Wright's*, 124. "The Rules of Syntax may all be included under three heads, *Concord*, *Government*, and *Position*."—*Bullions's E. Gram.*, p. 87. "*Position* means the *place* which a word occupies in a sentence."—*Ib.* "These rules may be mostly ranked under the two heads of *agreement* and *government*; the remainder may be termed *miscellaneous*."—*Nutting's Gram.*, p. 92. "Syntax treats of the agreement, government and proper arrangement of words in *a sentence*."—*Frost's El. of Gram.*, p. 43. This last-named author, in touching the text of my books, has often *corrupted* it, as he does here; but my definitions of *the tenses* he copied without marring them much. The borrowing occurred as early as 1828, and I add this notice now, lest any should suppose *me* the plagiarist.

OBS. 5.—Most of our English grammars have *more* rules of syntax than are needed, and yet are very deficient in *such* as are needed. To say, as some do, that articles, adjectives, and participles, *agree* with nouns, is to teach Greek or Latin syntax, and not English. To throw, as Nutting does, the whole syntax of adverbs into a remark on *such a rule of agreement,* is to choose disorder for its own sake. To say, with Frost, Hall, Smith, Perley, Kirkham, Sanborn, Rand, and others, "The nominative case *governs* the verb in number and person," and again, "A verb must *agree* with its nominative case in number and person," is to confound the meaning of *government* and *agreement,* to say the same thing in different words, and to leave the subject of a verb still without a rule: for rules of government are applicable only to the words governed, and nothing ever agrees with that which governs it.[325] To say, with Murray and others, "Participles have the same government as the verbs from which they are derived," is to say nothing by which either verbs or participles may be parsed, or any of their errors corrected: those many grammarians, therefore, who make this their only rule for participles, leave them all without any syntax. To say, with Murray, Alger, and others, "Adverbs, *though they have no government of case, tense, &c.,* require an appropriate *situation* in the sentence," is to squander words at random, and leave the important question unanswered, "To what do adverbs relate?" To say again, with the same gentlemen, "Conjunctions connect *the same moods and tenses of verbs, and cases* of nouns and pronouns," is to put an ungrammatical, obscure, and useless assertion, in the place of an important rule. To say merely, "Prepositions govern the objective case," is to rest all the syntax of prepositions on a rule that never applies to them, but which is meant only for one of the constructions of the objective case. To say, as many do, "Interjections *require* the objective case of a pronoun of the first person after them, and the nominative case of the second," is to tell what is utterly false as the words stand, and by no means true in the sense which the authors intend.

Finally, to suppose, with Murray, that, "the Interjection *does not require a distinct, appropriate rule*," is in admirable keeping with all the foregoing quotations, and especially with his notion of what it *does* require; namely, "the *objective case* of the first person:" but who dares deny that the following exclamation is good English?

"*O* wretched *we!* why were we hurried down This lubric and adulterate age!"—*Dryden*.

OBS. 6.—The *truth* of any doctrine in science, can be nothing else than its conformity to facts, or to the nature of things; and chiefly by what he knows of the things themselves, must any one judge of what others say concerning them. Erroneous or inadequate views, confused or inconsistent statements, are the peculiar property of those who advance them; they have, in reality, no relationship to science itself, because they originate in ignorance; but all science is knowledge—it is knowledge methodized. What general rules are requisite for the syntactical parsing of the several parts of speech in English, may be seen at once by any one who will consider for a moment the usual construction of each. The correction of false syntax, in its various forms, will require more—yes, five times as many; but such of these as answer only the latter purpose, are, I think, better reserved for notes under the principal rules. The doctrines which I conceive most worthy to form the leading canons of our syntax, are those which are expressed in the twenty-four rules above. If other authors prefer more, or fewer, or different principles for their chief rules, I must suppose, it is because they have studied the subject less. Biased, as we may be, both by our knowledge and by our ignorance, it is easy for men to differ respecting matters of *expediency*; but that clearness, order, and consistency, are both *expedient*, and *requisite*, in didactic compositions, is what none can doubt.

OBS. 7.—Those English grammarians who tell us, as above, that syntax is divided into *parts*, or included under a certain number of *heads*, have almost universally contradicted themselves by treating the subject without any regard to such a division; and, at the same time, not a few have somehow been led into the gross error of supposing broad principles of concord or government where no such things exist. For example, they have invented general RULES like these: "The adjective *agrees* with its noun in number, case, and gender."—*Bingham's English Gram.*, p. 40. "Interjections *govern* the nominative case, and sometimes the objective: as, 'O thou! alas me!'"—*Ib.*, p. 43. "Adjectives *agree* with their nouns in number."—*Wilbur and Livingston's Gram.*, p. 22. "Participles *agree* with their nouns in number."—*Ib.*, p. 23. "Every adjective *agrees in number* with some substantive expressed or understood."—*Hiley's Gram.*, Rule 8th, p. 77. "The article THE *agrees* with nouns in either number: as, *The wood, the woods.*"—*Bucke's Classical Grammar of the English Language*, p. 84. "O! oh! ah! *require* the accusative case of a pronoun in the first person after them: as '*Ah me!*' But when the second person is used, *it requires* a nominative case: as, '*O thou!*'"—*Ib.*, p. 87. "Two or more Nominatives in the singular number, connected by the Conjunction *or, nor*, EITHER, NEITHER, *govern* a singular Verb. But Pronouns singular, of different persons, joined by *or*, EITHER, *nor*, NEITHER, *govern* a plural Verb."—*Ib.*, p. 94. "One Nominative frequently *governs* many Verbs."—*Ib.*, p. 95. "Participles are sometimes *governed* by the article."—*Murray's Gram.*, 8vo, p. 192. "An adverb, an adjective, or a participle, may involve in itself the force of *a preposition, and govern* the objective case."—*Nutting's Gram.*, p. 99. "The nominative case *governs* the verb." [326]—*Greenleaf's Gram.*, p. 32; *Kirkham's*, 176; and others. "The nominative case *comes before* the verb."—*Bingham's Gram.*, p. 38; *Wilbur and Livingston's*, 23. "The Verb TO BE, *always governs* a Nominative, *unless it be* of the Infinitive Mood."—*Buchanan's Syntax*, p. 94. "A verb in the infinitive mood *may be governed* by a verb, noun, adjective, participle, or pronoun."—*Kirkham's Gram.*, p. 187. Or, (as a substitute for the foregoing rule,) say, according to this author: "A verb in the infinitive mood, *refers* to some noun or pronoun, as its subject or actor."—*Ib.*, p. 188. Now what does he know of English grammar, who supposes any of these rules to be worthy of the place which they hold, or have held, in the halls of instruction?

OBS. 8.—It is a very common fault with the compilers of English grammars, to join together in the same rule the syntax of different parts of speech, uniting laws that must ever be applied separately in parsing. For example: "RULE XI. Articles and adjectives *relate to nouns* expressed or understood; and the adjectives *this, that, one, two*, must agree in number with the nouns to which they relate."—*Comly's Gram.*, p. 87. Now, in parsing an *article*, why should the learner have to tell all this story about *adjectives*? Such a mode of expressing the rule, is certainly in bad taste; and, after all, the syntax of adjectives is not here comprised, for they often relate to pronouns. "RULE III. Every adjective and participle *belongs* to some noun or pronoun expressed or understood."—*Frost's El. of Gram.*, p. 44. Here a compiler who in his etymology supposes participles to be *verbs*, allows them no other construction than that of *adjectives*. His rule implicitly denies that they can either be parts of their verbs in the formation of *tenses*, or be governed by prepositions in the character of *gerunds*. To suppose that a *noun* may govern the objective case, is both absurd in itself, and contrary to all authority; yet, among his forty-nine rules, this author has the following: "RULE XXV. A participial *noun* is sometimes governed by a preposition, and *may govern an objective case*; as, 'George is too fond of *wasting time* in trifles.'"—*Frost's El. of Gram.*, p. 47. Here again is the fault of which I am speaking, two rules in one; and this fault is combined with an other still worse. *Wasting* is a participle, governed by *of*; and *time* is a *noun*, governed by *wasting*. The latter is a declinable word, and found in the objective case; the former is indeclinable, and found in no case. It is an error to suppose that cases are the only things which are susceptible of being governed; nor is the brief rule, "Prepositions govern the objective case," so very clear a maxim as never to be misapprehended. If the learner infer from it, that *all* prepositions must necessarily govern the objective case, or that the objective case *is always* governed by a preposition, he will be led into a great mistake.

OBS. 9.—This error of crowding things together, is still more conspicuous in the following examples: "RULE IV. Every article, adjective, and participle, *must qualify* some noun, or pronoun, either expressed or understood."—*Nutting's Gram.*, p. 94. "RULE IX. The objective case is governed by a transitive verb or a preposition, usually coming before it."—*Ib.*, p. 98. Here an author who separates participles from verbs, has attempted first to compress the entire syntax of three different parts of speech into one short rule; and, secondly, to embrace all the forms of dependence, incident to objective nouns and pronouns, in an other as short. This brevity is a poor exchange for the order and distribution which it prevents—especially as none of its objects are here reached. Articles do not relate to pronouns, unless the obsolete phrase *the which* is to be revived; [327] participles have other constructions than those which adjectives admit; there are exceptions to the rules which tie articles to nouns, and adjectives to nouns or pronouns; and the objective case may not only be governed by a participle, but may be put in apposition with an other objective. The objective case in English usually stands for the Latin genitive, dative, accusative, and ablative; hence any rule that shall embrace the whole construction of this one case, will be the sole counterpart to four fifths of all the rules in any code of Latin syntax. For I imagine the construction of these four oblique cases, will be found to occupy at least that proportion of the syntactical rules and notes in any Latin grammar that can be found. Such rules, however, are often placed under false or equivocal titles;[328] as if they contained the construction of the *governing* words, rather than that of the *governed*. And this latter error, again, has been transferred to most of our English grammars, to the exclusion of any rule for the proper construction of participles, of adverbs, of conjunctions, of prepositions, or of interjections. See the syntax of Murray and his copyists, whose treatment of these parts of speech is noticed in the fifth observation above.

OBS. 10.—It is doubtless most convenient, that, in all rules for the construction of *cases*, nouns and pronouns be taken together; because the very same doctrines apply equally well to both, and a case is as distinct a thing in the mind, as a part of speech. This method, therefore, I have myself pursued; and it has indeed the authority of all grammarians—not excepting those who violate its principles by adopting two special rules for the relative pronoun, which are not needed. These special rules, which I shall notice again hereafter, may be seen in Murray's Rule 6th, which is double, and contains them both. The most complex rule that I have admitted, is that which embraces the government of objectives by verbs and participles. The regimen by verbs, and the regimen by participles, may not improperly be reckoned distinct principles; but the near alliance of participles to their verbs, seems to be a sufficient reason for preferring one rule to two, in this instance.

OBS. 11.—An other common fault in the treatment of this part of grammar, is the practice of making many of the rules *double*, or even *triple*, in their form. Of L. Murray's twenty-two rules, for instance, there are six which severally consist of two distinct paragraphs; and one is composed of three such parts, with examples under each. Five others, though simple in their form, are complex in their doctrine, and liable to the objections which have been urged above against this characteristic. These twelve, therefore, I either reject entirely from my catalogue, or divide and simplify to fit them for their purpose. In short, by comparing the twenty-two rules which were adopted by this popular grammarian, with the twenty-four which are given in this work, the reader may see, that twelve of the former have pleased me too little to have any place at all among the latter, and that none of the remaining ten have been thought worthy to be copied without considerable alteration. Nor are the rules which I adopt, more nearly coincident with those of any other writer. I do not proffer to the schools the second-hand instructions of a mere compiler. In his twenty-two rules, independently of their examples, Hurray has used six hundred and seventeen words, thus giving an average of twenty-eight to each rule; whereas in the twenty-four rules which are presented above, the words are but four hundred and thirty-six, making the average less than nineteen. And yet I have not only divided some of his propositions and extended others, but, by rejecting what was useless or erroneous, and filling up the deficiencies which mark his code, I have delivered twice the amount of doctrine in two thirds of the space, and furnished eleven important rules which are not contained in his grammar. Thus much, in this place, to those who so frequently ask, "Wherein does your book differ from Murray's?"

OBS. 12.—Of all the systems of syntax, or of grammar, which it has been my fortune to examine, a book which was first published by Robinson and Franklin of New York in 1839, a fair-looking duodecimo volume of 384 pages, under the brief but rather ostentatious title, "THE GRAMMAR *of the English Language*" is, I think, the most faulty,—the most remarkable for the magnitude, multitude, and variety, of its strange errors, inconsistencies, and defects. This singular performance is the work of *Oliver B. Peirce*, an itinerant lecturer on grammar, who dates his preface at "Rome, N. Y., December 29th, 1838." Its leading characteristic is boastful innovation; it being fall of acknowledged "contempt for the works of other writers."—P. 379. It lays "claim to *singularity*" as a merit, and boasts of a new thing under the sun—"in a theory RADICALLY NEW, a Grammar of the English Language; something which I believe," says the author, "has NEVER

BEFORE BEEN FOUND."—P. 9. The old scholastic notion, that because Custom is the arbitress of speech, novelty is excluded from grammar, this hopeful reformer thoroughly condemns; "repudiating this sentiment to the full extent of it," (*ib.*) and "writing his theory as though he had never seen a book, entitled an English Grammar."—*Ib.* And, for all the ends of good learning, it would have been as well or better, if he never had. His passion for novelty has led him not only to abandon or misapply, in an unprecedented degree, the usual terms of the art, but to disregard in many instances its most unquestionable principles, universal as well as particular. His parts of speech are the following ten: "Names, Substitutes, *Asserters*, Adnames, Modifiers, Relatives, Connectives, Interrogatives, Repliers, and Exclamations."—*The Gram.*, p. 20. His *names* are nouns; his *substitutes* are pronouns, and any adjectives whose nouns are not expressed; his *asserters* are verbs and participles, though the latter assert nothing; his *adnames* are articles, adjectives whose nouns or pronouns are expressed, and adverbs that relate to adjectives; his *modifiers* are such adverbs as "modify the sense or sound of a whole sentence;" his *relatives* are prepositions, some of which *govern no object*; his *connectives* are conjunctions, with certain adverbs and phrases; his *interrogatives* and *repliers* are new parts of speech, very lamely explained; his *exclamations* are interjections, and "*phrases used independently*; as, O hapless choice!"—*The Gram.*, p. 22. In parsing, he finds a world of "*accommodatives*;" as, "John is *more than five years* older than William."—*Ib.* p. 202. Here he calls the whole phrase "*more than five years*" "a secondary *adname*" i. e., *adjective*. But, in the phrase, "*more than five years* afterwards," he would call the same words "a secondary *modifier*;" i. e., *adverb.*—*Ib.*, p. 203. And, in the phrase, "*more than five years* before the war," he would call them "a secondary *relative*;" i. e., *preposition.—Ib.*, p. 204. And so of other phrases innumerable. His cases are five, two of which are new, "the *Independent*" and "the *Twofold* case." His "*independent* case" is sometimes the nominative in form, as "*thou*" and "*she;*" (p. 62;) sometimes the objective, as, "*me*" and "*him;*" (p. 62 and p. 199;) sometimes erroneously supposed to be the subject of a finite verb; while *his nominative* is sometimes as erroneously said to have *no* verb. His code of syntax has two sorts of rules, Analytical and Synthetical. The former are professedly seventeen in number; but, many of them consisting of two, three, or four distinct parts, their real number is more properly thirty-four. The latter are reckoned forty-five; but if we count their separate parts, they are fifty-six: and these with the others make *ninety*. I shall not particularize their faults. All of them are whimsically conceived and badly written. In short, had the author artfully designed to turn English grammar into a subject of contempt and ridicule, by as ugly a caricature of it as he could possibly invent, he could never have hit the mark more exactly than he has done in this "*new theory*"—this rash production, on which he so sincerely prides himself. Alone as he is, in well-nigh all his opinions, behold how prettily he talks of "COMMON SENSE, the only sure foundation of any theory!" and says, "On this imperishable foundation—this rock of eternal endurance—I rear my superstructure, *the edifice of scientific truth*, the temple of Grammatical consistency!"—*Peirce's Preface*, p. 7.

OBS. 13.—For the teaching of different languages, it has been thought very desirable to have "a Series of grammars, Greek, Latin, English, &c., all, so far as general principles are concerned, upon the same plan, and as nearly in the same words as the genius of the languages would permit."—See *Bullions's Principles of E. Gram.*, 2d Ed., pp. iv and vi. This scheme necessarily demands a minute comparison not only of the several languages themselves, but also of the various grammars in which their principles, whether general or particular, are developed. For by no other means can it be ascertained to what extent uniformity of this kind will be either profitable to the learner, or consistent with truth. Some books have been published, which, it is pretended, are thus accommodated to one an other, and to the languages of which they treat. But, in view of the fact, that the Latin or the Greek grammars now extant, (to say nothing of the French, Spanish, and others,) are almost as various and as faulty as the English, I am apprehensive that this is a desideratum not soon to be realized,—a design more plausible in the prospectus, than feasible in the attempt. At any rate, the grammars of different languages must needs differ as much as do the languages themselves, otherwise some of their principles will of course be false; and we have already seen that the nonobservance of this has been a fruitful source of error in respect to English syntax. The achievement, however, is not altogether impossible, if a man of competent learning will devote to it a sufficient degree of labour. But the mere revising or altering of some one grammar in each language, can scarcely amount to any thing more than a pretence of improvement. Waiving the pettiness of compiling upon the basis of an other man's compilation, the foundation of a good grammar for any language, must be both deeper and broader than all the works which Professor Bullions has selected to build upon: for the Greek, than Dr. Moor's "*Elementa Linguæ, Græcæ;*" for the Latin, than Dr. Adam's "*Rudiments of Latin and English Grammar;*" for the English, than Murray's "*English Grammar,*" or Lennie's "*Principles of English Grammar;*" which last work, in fact, the learned gentleman preferred, though he pretends to have mended the code of Murray. But, certainly, Lennie never supposed himself a copyist of Murray; nor was he to much extent an imitator of him, either in method or in style.

OBS. 14.—We have, then, in this new American form of "*The Principles of English Grammar,*" Lennie's very compact little book, altered, enlarged, and bearing on its title-page (which is otherwise in the very words of Lennie) an other author's name, and, in its early editions, the false and self-accusing inscription, "(ON THE PLAN OF MURRAY'S GRAMMAR.)" And this work, claiming to have been approved "by the most competent judges," now challenges the praise not only of being "better adapted to the use of academies and schools *than any yet published*" but of so presenting "*the rules and principles of general grammar*, as that they may apply to, and be in perfect harmony with, *the grammars of the dead languages*"—*Recommendations*, p. iv. These are admirable professions for a critical author to publish; especially, as every rule or principle of General Grammar, condemning as it must whoever violates it, cannot but "be in *perfect harmony* with" every thing that is true. In this model for all grammars, Latin, Greek, &c., the doctrines of punctuation, of abbreviations, and of capital letters, and also sections on the rhetorical divisions of a discourse, the different kinds of composition, the different kinds of prose composition, and the different kinds of poetry, are made *parts of the Syntax*; while his hints for correct and elegant writing, and his section on the composition of letters and themes, which other writers suppose to belong rather to syntax, are here subjoined as *parts of Prosody*. In the exercises for parsing appended to his *Etymology*, the Doctor furnishes *twenty-five Rules of Syntax*, which, he says, "are not intended to be committed to memory, but to be used as directions to the beginner in parsing the exercises under them."—*E. Gram.*, p. 75. Then, for his syntax proper, he copies from Lennie, with some alterations, *thirty-four other rules*, nine of which are double, and all are jumbled together by both authors, without any regard to the distinction of concord and government, so common in the grammars of the dead languages, and even, so far as I can discover, without any principle of arrangement whatever. They profess indeed to have placed those rules first, which are eaisest [sic—KTH] to learn, and oftenest to be applied; but the syntax of *articles*, which even on this principle should have formed the first of the series, is placed by Lennie as the thirty-fourth rule, and by his amender as the thirty-second. To all this complexity the latter adds *twenty-two Special Rules*, with an abundance of "*Notes*" "*Observations*" and "*Remarks*" distinguished by these titles, on some principle which no one but the author can understand. Lastly, his *method of syntactical parsing* is not only mixed up with etymological questions and answers, but his *directions* for it, with their *exemplification,* are perplexingly at variance with his own *specimen* of the performance. See his book, pages 131 and 133. So much for this grand scheme.

OBS. 15.—Strictures like the foregoing, did they not involve the defence of grammar itself, so as to bear upon interests more important than the success or failure of an elementary book, might well be withheld through motives of charity, economy, and peace. There is many a grammar now extant, concerning which a truly critical reader may know more at first sight, than ever did he that made it. What such a reader will be inclined to rate beneath criticism, an other perhaps will confidently pronounce above it. If my remarks are just, let the one approve them for the other's sake. For what becomes of the teaching of grammar, when that which is received as the most excellent method, must be exempted from censure by reason of its utter worthlessness? And what becomes of Universal Syntax, when the imperfect systems of the Latin and Greek grammars, in stead of being amended, are modelled to the grossest faults of what is worthless in our own?[329]

OBS. 16.—What arrangement of Latin or Greek syntax may be best in itself, I am not now concerned to show. Lily did not divide his, as others have divided the subject since; but first stated briefly his *three concords,* and then proceeded to what he called *the construction* of the several parts of speech, taking them in their order. The three concords of Lily are the following: (1.) Of the *Nominative and Verb;* to which the accusative before an infinitive, and the collective noun with a plural verb, are reckoned exceptions; while the agreement of a verb or pronoun with two or more nouns, is referred to the figure *syllepsis.* (2.) Of the *Substantive and Adjective;* under which the agreement of participles, and of some pronouns, is placed in the form of a note. (3.) Of the *Relative and Antecedent;* after which the two special rules for the *cases* of relatives are given as underparts. Dr. Adam divided his syntax into two parts; of Simple Sentences, and of Compound Sentences. His three concords are the following: (1.) Of one *Substantive with an Other*; which construction is placed by Lily and many others among the figures of syntax, and is called *apposition*. (2.) Of an *Adjective with a Substantive*; under which principle, we are told to take adjective pronouns and participles. (3.) Of a *Verb with a Nominative*; under which, the collective noun with a verb of either number, is noticed in an observation. The construction of relatives, of conjunctions, of comparatives, and of words put absolute, this author reserves for the second part of his syntax; and the agreement of plural verbs or pronouns with joint nominatives or antecedents, which Ruddiman places in an observation on his *four concords*, is here absurdly reckoned a part of the construction of conjunctions. Various divisions and subdivisions of the Latin syntax, with special dispositions of some particular principles of it, may be seen in the elaborate grammars of Despauter, Prat, Ruddiman, Grant, and other writers. And here it may be proper to observe, that, the mixing of syntax with etymology, after the manner of Ingersoll, Kirkham, R. W. Green, R. C. Smith, Sanborn, Felton, Hazen, Parkhurst, Parker and Fox, Weld, and others, is a modern innovation, pernicious to both; either topic being sufficiently comprehensive, and sufficiently difficult, when they are treated separately; and each having, in some instances, employed the pens of able writers almost to the exclusion of the other.

OBS. 17.—The syntax of any language must needs conform to the peculiarities of its etymology, and also be consistent with itself; for all will expect better things of a scholar, than to lay down positions in one part of his grammar, that are irreconcilable with what he has stated in an other. The English language, having few inflections, has also few concords or agreements, and still fewer governments. Articles, adjectives, and participles, which in many other languages agree with their nouns in gender, number, and case, have usually, in English, no modifications in which they *can agree* with their nouns. Yet *Lowth* says, "The adjective in English, having no variation of gender and number, *cannot but agree* with the substantive in these respects."—*Short Introd. to Gram.*, p. 86. What then is the *agreement* of words? Can it be anything else than their *similarity* in some common property or modification? And is it not obvious, that no two things in nature can at all *agree*, or *be alike*, except in some quality or accident which belongs to each of them? Yet how often have *Murray* and others, as well as *Lowth*, forgotten this! To give one instance out of many: "*Gender* has respect only to the third person singular of the pronouns, *he, she, it.*"—*Murray, J. Peirce, Flint, Lyon, Bacon, Russell, Fisk, Maltby, Alger, Miller, Merchant, Kirkham*, and other careless copyists. Yet, according to these same gentlemen, "Gender is *the distinction of nouns*, with regard to sex;" and, "Pronouns *must always agree* with their antecedents, *and the nouns* for which they stand, in gender." Now, not one of these three careless assertions can possibly be reconciled with either of the others!

OBS. 18.—*Government* has respect only to nouns, pronouns, verbs, participles, and prepositions; the other five parts of speech neither govern nor are governed. The *governing* words may be either nouns, or verbs, or participles, or prepositions; the words *governed* are either nouns, or pronouns, or verbs, or participles. In parsing, the learner must remember that the rules of government are not to be applied to the *governing* words, but to those which *are governed*; and which, for the sake of brevity, are often technically named after the particular form or modification assumed; as, *possessives, objectives, infinitives, gerundives*. These are the only things in English, that can properly be said to be subject to government; and these are always so, in their own names; unless we except such infinitives as stand in the place of nominatives. *Gerundives* are participles governed by prepositions; but, there being little or no occasion to distinguish these from other participles, we seldom use this name. The Latin *Gerund* differs from a participle, and the English *Gerundive* differs from a participial noun. The participial noun may be the subject or the object of a verb, or may govern the possessive case before it, like any other noun; but the true English gerundive, being essentially a participle, and governing an object after it, like any other participle, is itself governed only by a preposition. At least, this is its usual and allowed construction, and no other is acknowledged to be indisputably right.

OBS. 19.—The simple *Relations* of words in English, (or those several *uses* of the parts of speech which we may refer to this head,) are the following nine: (1.) Of Articles to nouns, by Rule 1st; (2.) Of Nominatives to verbs, by Rule 2d; (3.) Of Nominatives absolute or independent, by Rule 8th; (4.) Of Adjectives to nouns or pronouns, by Rule 9th; (5.) Of Participles to nouns or pronouns, by Rule 20th; (6.) Of Adverbs to verbs, participles, &c., by Rule 21st; (7.) Of Conjunctions as connecting words, phrases, or sentences, by Rule 22nd; (8.) Of Prepositions as showing the relations of things, by Rule 23d; (9.) Of Interjections as being used independently, by Rule 24th.

OBS. 20.—The syntactical *Agreements* in English, though actually much fewer than those which occur in Latin, Greek, or French, may easily be so reckoned as to amount to double, or even triple, the number usually spoken of by the old grammarians. The twenty-four rules above, embrace the following ten heads, which may not improperly be taken for so many distinct concords: (1.) Of a Noun or Pronoun in direct apposition with another, by Rule 3d; (2.) Of a Noun or Pronoun after a verb or participle not transitive, by Rule 6th; (3.) Of a Pronoun with its antecedent, by Rule 10th; (4.) Of a Pronoun with a collective noun, by Rule 11th; (5.) Of a Pronoun with joint antecedents, by Rule 12th; (6.) Of a Pronoun with disjunct antecedents, by Rule 13th; (7.) Of a Verb with its nominative, by Rule 14th;

(8.) Of a Verb with a collective noun, by Rule 15th; (9.) Of a Verb with joint nominatives, by Rule 16th; (10.) Of a Verb with disjunct nominatives, by Rule 17th. To these may be added two other *special* concords, less common and less important, which will be explained in *notes* under the rules: (11.) Of one Verb with an other, in mood, tense, and form, when two are connected so as to agree with the same nominative; (12.) Of Adjectives that imply unity or plurality, with their nouns, in number.

OBS. 21.—Again, by a different mode of reckoning them, the concords or the *general principles* of agreement, in our language, may be made to be only three or four; and some of these much *less general*, than they are in other languages: (1.) *Words in apposition agree in case*, according to Rule 3d; of which principle, Rule 6th may be considered a modification. (2.) *Pronouns agree, with their nouns, in person, number, and gender*, according to Rule 10th; of which principle, Rules 11th, 12th, and 13th, may be reckoned modifications. (3.) *Verbs agree with their nominatives, in person and number*, according to Rule 14th; of which principle Rules 15th, 16th, and 17th, and the occasional agreement of one verb with an other, may be esteemed mere modifications. (4.) *Some adjectives agree with their nouns in number*. These make up the twelve concords above enumerated.

OBS. 22.—The rules of *Government* in the best Latin grammars are about sixty; and these are usually distributed (though not very properly) under three heads; "1. Of Nouns. 2. Of Verbs. 3. Of Words indeclinable."—*Grant's Lat. Gram.*, p. 170. "Regimen est triplex: 1. Nominum. 2. Verborum. 3. Vocum indeclinabilium."—*Ruddiman's Gram.*, p. 138. This division of the subject brings all the *titles* of the rules wrong. For example, if the rule be, "Active verbs govern the accusative case," this is not properly "the government of *verbs*" but rather the government *of the accusative* by verbs. At least, such titles are *equivocal*, and likely to mislead the learner. The governments in English are only seven, and these are expressed, perhaps with sufficient distinctness, in six of the foregoing rules: (1.) Of Possessives by nouns, in Rule 4th; (2.) Of Objectives by verbs, in Rule 5th; (3.) Of Objectives by participles, in Rule 5th; (4.) Of Objectives by prepositions, in Rule 7th; (5.) Of Infinitives by the preposition *to*, in Rule 18th; (6.) Of Infinitives by the verbs *bid, dare*, &c., in Rule 19th; (7.) Of Participles by prepositions, in Rule 20th.

OBS. 23.—The *Arrangement* of words, (which will be sufficiently treated of in the observations hereafter to be made on the several rules of construction,) is an important part of syntax, in which not only the beauty but the propriety of language is intimately concerned, and to which particular attention should therefore be paid in composition. But it is to be remembered, that the mere collocation of words in a sentence never affects the method of parsing them: on the contrary, the same words, however placed, are always to be parsed in precisely the same way, so long as they express precisely the same meaning. In order to show that we have parsed any part of an inverted or difficult sentence rightly, we are at liberty to declare the meaning by any arrangement which will make the construction more obvious, provided we retain both the sense and all the words unaltered; but to drop or alter any word, is to pervert the text under pretence of resolving it, and to make a mockery of parsing. Grammar rightly learned, enables one to understand both the sense and the construction of whatsoever is rightly written; and he who reads what he does not understand, reads to little purpose. With great indignity to the muses, several pretenders to grammar have foolishly taught, that, "In parsing poetry, in order to *come at the meaning* of the author, the learner will find it necessary to transpose his language."—*Kirkham's Gram.*, p. 166. See also the books of *Merchant, Wilcox, O. B. Peirce, Hull, Smith, Felton*, and others, to the same effect. To what purpose can he *transpose* the words of a sentence, who does not first see what they mean, and how to explain or parse them as they stand?

OBS. 24.—Errors innumerable have been introduced into the common modes of parsing, through a false notion of what constitutes a *simple sentence*. Lowth, Adam, Murray, Gould, Smith, Ingersoll, Comly, Lennie, Hiley, Bullions, Wells, and many others, say, "A simple sentence has in it *but one subject*, and *one finite verb*: as, 'Life is short.'"—*L. Murray's Gram.*, p. 141. In accordance with this assertion, some assume, that, "Every nominative *has its own verb* expressed or understood;" and that, "Every verb (except in the infinitive mood and participle) *has its own nominative* expressed or understood."—*Bullions's E. Gram.*, p. 87. The adopters of these dogmas, of course think it right to *supply* a nominative whenever they do not find a separate one expressed for every finite verb, and a verb whenever they do not find a separate one expressed for every nominative. This mode of interpretation not only precludes the agreement of a verb with two or more nominatives, so as to render nugatory two of the most important rules of these very gentlemen's syntax; but, what is worse, it perverts many a plain, simple, and perfect sentence, to a form which its author did not choose, and a meaning which he never intended. Suppose, for example, the text to be, "A good constitution and good laws make good subjects."—*Webster's Essays*, p. 152. Does not the verb *make* agree with *constitution* and *laws*, taken conjointly? and is it not a *perversion* of the sentence to interpret it otherwise? Away then with all this *needless subaudition!* But while we thus deny that there can be a true ellipsis of what is not necessary to the construction, it is not to be denied that there *are* true ellipses, and in some men's style very many. The assumption of O. B. Peirce, that no correct sentence is elliptical, and his impracticable project of a grammar founded on this principle, are among the grossest of possible absurdities.

OBS. 25.—Dr. Wilson says, "There may be several subjects to the same verb, several verbs to the same subject, or several objects to the same verb, and the sentence be simple. But when the sentence remains simple, the same verb must be differently affected by its several adjuncts, or the sense liable to be altered by a separation. If the verb or the subject *be* affected in the same manner, or the sentence *is* resolvable into more, it is compounded. Thus, 'Violet, indigo, blue, green, yellow, orange, and red, mixed in due proportion, produce white,' is a simple sentence, for the subject is indivisible. But, 'Violet, indigo, blue, green, yellow, orange, and red, are refrangible rays of light,' is a compound sentence, and may be separated into seven."—*Essay on Gram.*, p. 186. The propriety of the distinction here made, is at least questionable; and I incline to consider the second example a simple sentence, as well as the first; because what the writer calls a separation into seven, involves a change of *are* to *is*, and of *rays* to *ray*, as well as a sevenfold repetition of this altered predicate, "*is a refrangible ray of light*." But the parser, in interpreting the words of others, and expounding the construction of what is written, has no right to alter anything in this manner. Nor do I admit that he has a right to insert or repeat anything *needlessly*; for the nature of a sentence, or the syntax of some of its words, may often be altered without change of the sense, or of any word for an other: as, "'A wall seven feet high;' that is, 'A wall *which is* seven feet high.'"—*Hiley's Gram.*, p. 109. "'He spoke and acted prudently;' that is, 'He spoke *prudently*, and *he* acted prudently.'"—*Ibid.* "'He spoke and acted wisely;' that is, 'He spoke *wisely*, and *he* acted wisely.'"—*Murray's Gram.*, p. 219; *Alger's*, 70: *R. C. Smith's*, 183; *Weld's*, 192; and others. By this notion of ellipsis, the connexion or joint relation of words is destroyed.

OBS. 26.—Dr. Adam, who thought the division of sentences into simple and compound, of sufficient importance to be made the basis of a general division of syntax into two parts, has defined a simple sentence to be, "that which has but one nominative, and one finite verb;" and a compound sentence, "that which has more than one nominative, or one finite verb." And of the latter he gives the following erroneous and self-contradictory account: "A compound sentence is made up of two or more simple sentences or *phrases*, and is commonly called a *Period*. The parts of which a compound sentence consists, are called *Members* or *Clauses*. In every compound sentence there are either several subjects and one attribute, or several attributes and one subject, or both several subjects and several attributes; that is, there are either several nominatives applied to the same verb, or several verbs applied to the same nominative, or both. Every verb marks a judgment or attribute, and every attribute must have a subject. There must, therefore, be in every sentence or period, as many propositions as there are verbs of a finite mode. Sentences are compounded by means of relatives and conjunctions; as, Happy is the man *who* loveth religion, and practiseth virtue."—*Adam's Gram.*, p. 202; *Gould's*, 199; and others.

OBS. 27.—Now if every compound sentence consists of such parts, members, or clauses, as are in themselves sentences, either simple or compound, either elliptical or complete; it is plain, in the first place, that the term "phrases" is misapplied above, because a phrase is properly only a part of some simple sentence. And if "a simple sentence is that which has but one nominative and one finite verb," and "a compound sentence is made up of two or more simple sentences," it follows, since "all sentences are either simple or compound," that, *in no sentence, can there be* "either several nominatives applied to the same verb, or several verbs applied to the same nominative." What, therefore, this author regarded as *the characteristic* of all compound sentences, is, according to his own previous positions, utterly impossible to any sentence. Nor is it less repugnant to his subsequent doctrine, that, "Sentences are compounded by means of *relatives* and *conjunctions*;" for, according to his notion, "A conjunction is an indeclinable word, which serves to join *sentences* together."—*Adam's Gram.*, p. 149. It is assumed, that, "In every *sentence* there must be a verb and a nominative expressed or understood."—*Ib.*, p. 151. Now if there happen to be two nominatives to one verb, as when it was said, "Even the *winds* and the *sea* obey him;" this cannot be anything more than a simple sentence; because one single verb is a thing indivisible, and how can we suppose it to form the most essential part of two different sentences at once?

OBS. 28.—The distinction, or real difference, between those simple sentences in which two or more nominatives or verbs are taken conjointly, and those compound sentences in which there is an ellipsis of some of the nominatives or verbs, is not always easy to be known or fixed; because in many instances, a supposed *ellipsis*, without at all affecting the sense, may obviously change the construction, and consequently the nature of the sentence. For example: "And they all forsook him, and [they all] fled."—*Mark*, xiv, 50. Some will say, that the words in brackets are here *understood*. I may deny it, because they are needless; and nothing needless can form a true ellipsis. To the supplying of useless words, if we admit the principle, there may be no end; and the notion that conjunctions join sentences only, opens a wide door for it. For example: "And that man was perfect and upright, and one that feared God, and eschewed evil."—*Job*, i, 1. No additional words will make this clause any plainer, and none are really necessary to the construction; yet some grammarians will parse it with the following impletions, or more: "And that man was *a* perfect *man*, and *he was an* upright *man*, and *he was* one *man* that feared God, and *that* eschewed evil *things*." It is easy to see how this liberty of interpretation, or of interpolation, will change simple sentences to compound sentences, as well as alter the nature and relation of many particular words; and at the same time, it takes away totally those peculiarities of construction by which Dr. Adam and others would recognize a sentence as being compound. What then? are there not two kinds of sentences? Yes, truly; but these authors are wrong in their notions and definitions of both. Joint nominatives or joint verbs may occur in either; but they belong primarily to some simple

THE ANALYZING OF SENTENCES.

To analyze a sentence, is, to resolve it into some species of constituent parts, but most properly into words, its first significant elements, and to point out their several relations and powers in the given connexion.

The component parts of a sentence are *members, clauses, phrases,* or *words*. Some sentences, which are short and simple, can only be divided into their words; others, which are long and complex, may be resolved into parts again and again divisible.

Of analysis applicable to sentences, there are several different methods; and, so far as their difference may compatibly aid the application of different principles of the science of grammar, there may be an advantage in the occasional use of each.

FIRST METHOD OF ANALYSIS.

Sentences not simple may be reduced to their constituent members, clauses, or simple sentences; and the means by which these are united, may be shown. Thus:—

EXAMPLE ANALYZED.

"Even the Atheist, who tells us that the universe is self-existent and indestructible—even he, who, instead of seeing the traces of a manifold wisdom in its manifold varieties, sees nothing in them all but the exquisite structures and the lofty dimensions of materialism—even he, who would despoil creation of its God, cannot look upon its golden suns, and their accompanying systems, without the solemn impression of a magnificence that fixes and overpowers him."—DR. CHALMERS, *Discourses on Revelation and Astronomy*, p. 231.

ANALYSIS.—This is a compound sentence, consisting of three complex members, which are separated by the two dashes. The three members are united in one sentence, by a suspension of the sense at each dash, and by two virtual repetitions of the subject, "*Atheist*" through the pronoun "*he*," put in the same case, and representing this noun. The sense mainly intended is not brought out till the period ends. Each of the three members is complex, because each has not only a relative clause, commencing with "*who*," but also an antecedent word which makes sense with "*cannot look*," &c. The first of these relative clauses involves also a subordinate, supplementary clause,—"*the universe is self-existent and indestructible*"—introduced after the verb "*tells*" by the conjunction "*that*." The last phrase, "*without the solemn impression*," &c., which is subjoined by "*without*" to "*cannot look*," embraces likewise a subordinate, relative clause,—"*that fixes and overpowers him*,"—which has two verbs; the whole, antecedent and all, being but an adjunct of an adjunct, yet an essential element of the sentence.

SECOND METHOD OF ANALYSIS.

Simple sentences, or the simple members of compound sentences, may be resolved into their PRINCIPAL and their SUBORDINATE PARTS; the subject, the verb, and the case put after or governed by the verb, being first pointed out as THE PRINCIPAL PARTS; and the other words being then detailed as ADJUNCTS to these, according to THE SENSE, or as adjuncts to adjuncts. Thus:—

EXAMPLE ANALYZED.

"Fear naturally quickens the flight of guilt. Rasselas could not catch the fugitive, with his utmost efforts; but, resolving to weary, by perseverance, him whom he could not surpass in speed, he pressed on till the foot of the mountain stopped his course."—DR. JOHNSON, *Rasselas*, p. 23.

ANALYSIS.—The first period here is a simple sentence. Its principal parts are—*Fear, quickens, flight*; *Fear* being the subject, *quickens* the verb, and *flight* the object. *Fear* has no adjunct; *naturally* is an adjunct of *quickens*; *the* and *of guilt* are adjuncts of *flight*. The second period is composed of several clauses, or simple members, united. The first of these is also a simple sentence, having, three principal parts—*Rasselas, could catch*, and *fugitive*; the subject, the verb, and its object, in their order. *Not* is added to *could catch*, reversing the meaning; *the* is an adjunct to *fugitive*; *with* joins its phrase to *could not catch*; but *his* and *utmost* are adjuncts of *efforts*. The word *but* connects the two chief members as parts of one sentence. "Resolving to weary" is an adjunct to the pronoun *he*, which stands before *pressed*. "By perseverance," is an adjunct to *weary*. *Him* is governed by *weary*, and is the antecedent to *whom*. "Whom he could not surpass in speed," is a relative clause, or subordinate simple member, having three principal parts—*he, could surpass*, and *whom*. *Not* and *in speed* are adjuncts to the verb *could surpass*. "He pressed on" is an other simple member, or sentence, and the chief clause here used, the others being subjoined to this. Its principal parts are two, *he* and *pressed*; the latter taking the particle *on* as an adjunct, and being intransitive. The words dependent on the nominative *he*, (to wit, *resolving, &c.,*) have already been mentioned. *Till* is a conjunctive adverb of time, connecting the concluding clause to *pressed on*. "The foot of the mountain stopped his course," is a subordinate clause and simple member, whose principal parts are—the subject *foot*, the verb *stopped*, and the object *course*. The adjuncts of *foot* are *the* and *of the mountain*; the verb in this sentence has no adjunct but *course*, which is better reckoned a principal word; lastly, *his* is an adjunct to *course*, and governed by it.

THIRD METHOD OF ANALYSIS.

Sentences may be partially analyzed by a resolution into their SUBJECTS and their PREDICATES, a method which some late grammarians have borrowed from the logicians; the grammatical subject with its adjuncts, being taken for the logical subject; and the finite verb, which some call the grammatical predicate[330] being, with its subsequent case and the adjuncts of both, denominated the predicate, or the logical predicate. Thus:—

EXAMPLE ANALYZED.

"Such is the emptiness of human enjoyment, that we are always impatient of the present. Attainment is followed by neglect, and possession, by disgust. Few moments are more pleasing than those in which the mind is concerting measures for a new undertaking. From the first hint that wakens the fancy, to the hour of actual execution, all is improvement and progress, triumph and felicity."—DR. JOHNSON, *Rambler*.

ANALYSIS.—Here the first period is a compound sentence, containing two clauses,—which are connected by *that*. In the first clause, *emptiness* is the grammatical subject, and "*the emptiness of human enjoyment*" is the logical. *Is* some would call the grammatical predicate, and "Such is," or *is such*, the logical; but the latter consists, as the majority teach, of "the copula" *is*, and "the attribute," or "predicate," *such*. In the second clause, (which explains the import of "*Such*,") the subject is *we*; which is unmodified, and in which therefore the logical form and the grammatical coincide and are the same. *Are* may here be called the grammatical predicate; and "*are always impatient of the present,*" the logical. The second period, too, is a compound sentence, having two clauses, which are connected by *and*. *Attainment* is the subject of the former; and, "*is followed by neglect*" is the predicate. In the latter, *possession* alone is the subject; and, "[*is followed*] *by disgust,*" is the predicate; the verb *is followed* being understood at the comma. The third period, likewise, is a compound, having three parts, with the two connectives *than* and *which*. Here we have *moments* for the first grammatical subject, and *Few moments* for the logical; then, *are* for the grammatical predicate, and *are more pleasing* for the logical: or, if we choose to say so, for "the copula and the attribute." "*Than those,*" is an elliptical member, meaning, "than *are* those *moments,*" or, "than those *moments are pleasing;*" both subject and predicate are wholly suppressed, except that *those* is reckoned a part of the logical subject. *In which* is an adjunct of *is concerting*, and serves well to connect the members, because *which* represents *those*, i.e. *those moments. Mind*, or *the mind*, is the next subject of affirmation; and *is concerting*, or, "*is concerting measures for a new undertaking,*" is the predicate or matter affirmed. Lastly, the fourth period, like the rest, is compound. The phrases commencing with *From* and *to*, describe a period of time, and are adjuncts of the verb *is*. The former contains a subordinate relative clause, of which *that* (representing *hint*) is the subject, and *wakens*, or *wakens the fancy*, the predicate. Of the principal clause, the word *all*, taken as a noun, is the subject, whether grammatical or logical; and "the copula," or "grammatical predicate," *is*, becomes, with its adjuncts and the nominatives following, the logical predicate.

FOURTH METHOD OF ANALYSIS.

All syntax is founded on the RELATION *of words one to an other, and the* CONNEXION *of clauses and phrases, according to* THE SENSE. *Hence sentences may be, in some sort, analyzed, and perhaps profitably, by the tracing of such relation or connexion, from link to link, through a series of words, beginning and ending with such as are somewhat remote from each other, yet within the period. Thus:—*

EXAMPLES ANALYZED.

1. "Swift would say, 'The thing has not life enough in it to keep it sweet;' Johnson, 'The creature possesses not vitality sufficient to preserve it from putrefaction.'"—MATT. HARRISON, *on the English Language*, p. 102. ANALYSIS.—What is the general sense of this passage? and what, the chain of connexion between the words *Swift* and *putrefaction*? The period is designed to show, that Swift preferred words of Saxon origin; and Johnson, of Latin. It has in contrast two coördinate members, tacitly connected: the verb *would say* being understood after *Johnson*, and perhaps also the particle *but*, after the semicolon. *Swift* is the subject of *would say*; and *would say* introduces the clause after it, as what would be said. *The* relates to *thing*; *thing* is the subject of *has*; *has*, which is qualified by *not*, governs *life*; *life* is qualified by the adjective *enough*, and by the phrase, *in it*; *enough* is the prior term of *to*; *to* governs *keep*; *keep* governs *it*, which stands for *the thing*; and *it*, in lieu of *the thing*, is qualified by *sweet*. The chief members are connected either by standing in contrast as members, or by *but*, understood before *Johnson*. *Johnson* is the subject of *would say*, understood: and this *would say*, again introduces a clause, as what would be said. *The* relates to *creature*; *creature* is the subject of *possesses*; *possesses*, which is qualified by *not*, governs *vitality*; *vitality* is qualified by *sufficient*; *sufficient* is the prior term of *to*; *to* governs *preserve*; *preserve* governs *it*, and is the prior term of *from*; and *from* governs *putrefaction*.

2. "There is one Being to whom we can look with a perfect conviction of finding that security, which nothing about us can give, and which nothing

about us can take away."—GREENWOOD; *Wells's School Gram.*, p. 192. [331]

ANALYSIS.—What is the general structure of this passage? and what, the chain of connexion "between the words *away* and *is?*" The period is a complex sentence, having four clauses, all connected together by relatives; the second, by *whom*, to the first and chief clause, *"There is one Being;"* the third and the fourth, to the second, by *which* and *which*; but the last two, having the same antecedent, *security,* and being coördinate, are also connected one to the other by *and.* As to "the chain of connexion," *Away* relates to *can take*; *can take* agrees with its nominative *nothing*, and governs *which*; *which* represents *security*; *security* is governed by *finding*; *finding* is governed by *of*; *of* refers back to *conviction*; *conviction* is governed by *with*; *with* refers back to *can look*; *can look* agrees with *we*, and is, in sense, the antecedent of *to*; *to* governs *whom*; *whom* represents *Being*; and *Being* is the subject of *is.*

FIFTH METHOD OF ANALYSIS.

The best and most thorough method of analysis is that of COMPLETE SYNTACTICAL PARSING; *a method which, for the sake of order and brevity, should ever be kept free from all mixture of etymological definitions or reasons, but which may be preceded or followed by any of the foregoing schemes of resolution, if the teacher choose to require any such preliminary or subsidiary exposition. This method is fully illustrated in the Twelfth Praxis below.*

OBSERVATIONS ON METHODS OF ANALYSIS.

OBS. 1.—The almost infinite variety in the forms of sentences, will sometimes throw difficulty in the way of the analyzer, be his scheme or his skill what it may. The last four or five observations of the preceding series have shown, that the distinction of sentences as *simple* or *compound*, which constitutes the chief point of the First Method of Analysis above, is not always plain, even to the learned. The definitions and examples which I have given, will make it *generally* so; and, where it is otherwise, the question or puzzle, it is presumed, cannot often be of much practical importance. If the difference be not obvious, it can hardly be a momentous error, to mistake a phrase for an elliptical clause, or to call such a clause a phrase.

OBS. 2.—The Second Method above is, I think, easier of application than any of the rest; and, if other analysis than the regular method of parsing seem desirable, this will probably be found as useful as any. There is, in many of our popular grammars, some recognition of the principles of this analysis—some mention of "the *principal parts* of a sentence," in accordance with what are so called above,—and also, in a few, some succinct account of the parts called "*adjuncts*;" but there seems to have been no prevalent practice of applying these principles, in any stated or well-digested manner. Lowth, Murray, Alger, W. Allen, Hart, Hiley, Ingersoll, Wells, and others, tell of these "PRINCIPAL PARTS;"—Lowth calling them, "the *agent*, the *attribute*, and the *object*;" (*Gram.*, p. 72;)—Murray, and his copyists, Alger, Ingersoll, and others, calling them, "the *subject*, the *attribute*, and the *object*;"—Hiley and Hart calling them, "the *subject* or *nominative*, the *attribute* or *verb*, and the *object*;"—Allen calling them, "the *nominative*, the *verb*, and (if the verb is active,) the *accusative* governed by the verb;" and also saying, "The nominative is sometimes called the *subject*; the verb, the *attribute*; and the accusative, the *object*;"—Wells calling them, "the *subject* or *nominative*, the *verb*, and the *object*;" and also recognizing the "*adjuncts*," as a species which "embraces all the words of a simple sentence [,] except the *principal parts*;"—yet not more than two of them all appearing to have taken any thought, and they but little, about the formal *application* of their common doctrine. In Allen's English Grammar, which is one of the best, and likewise in Wells's, which is equally prized, this reduction of all connected words, or parts of speech, into "the principal parts" and "the adjuncts," is fully recognized; the adjuncts, too, are discriminated by Allen, as "either primary or secondary," nor are their more particular species or relations overlooked; but I find no method prescribed for the analysis intended, except what Wells adopted in his early editions but has since changed to an other or abandoned, and no other allusion to it by, Allen, than this Note, which, with some appearance of intrusion, is appended to his "Method of Parsing the Infinitive Mood:"—"The pupil *may now begin* to analyse [*analyze*] the sentences, by distinguishing the principal words and their adjuncts."—*W. Allen's E. Gram.*, p. 258.

OBS. 3.—These authors in general, and many more, tell us, with some variation of words, that the agent, subject, or nominative, is that of which something is said, affirmed, or denied; that the attribute, verb, or predicate, is that which is said, affirmed, or denied, of the subject; and that the object, accusative, or case sequent, is that which is introduced by the finite verb, or affected by the action affirmed. Lowth says, "In English the nominative case, denoting the agent, usually goes before the verb, or attribution; and the objective case, denoting the object, follows the verb active."—*Short Introd.*, p. 72. Murray copies, but not literally, thus: "The nominative denotes the subject, and usually goes before the verb [,] or attribute; and the word *or phrase,* denoting the object, follows the verb: as, 'A wise man governs his passions.' Here, a *wise man* is the subject; *governs,* the attribute, or thing affirmed; and *his passions,* the object."—*Murray's Octavo*, p. 142; *Duodecimo,* 116. To include thus the adjuncts with their principals, as the logicians do, is *here* manifestly improper; because it unites what the grammatical analyzer is chiefly concerned to separate, and tends to defeat the main purpose for which "THE PRINCIPAL PARTS" are so named and distinguished.

OBS. 4.—The Third Method of Analysis, described above, is an attempt very briefly to epitomize the chief elements of a great scheme,—to give, in a nutshell, the substance of what our grammarians have borrowed from the logicians, then mixed with something of their own, next amplified with small details, and, in some instances, branched out and extended to enormous bulk and length. Of course, they have not failed to set forth the comparative merits of this scheme in a sufficiently favourable light. The two ingenious gentlemen who seem to have been chiefly instrumental in making it popular, say in their preface, "The rules of syntax contained in this work result directly from the analysis of propositions, and of compound sentences; and for this reason the student should make himself perfectly familiar with the sections relating to *subject* and *predicate*, and should be able readily to analyze sentences, whether simple or compound, and to explain their structure and connection. * * * This exercise *should always precede* the more minute and subsidiary labor of parsing. If the latter be conducted, as it often is, independently of previous analysis, the *principal advantage* to be derived from the study of language, as an intellectual exercise, will inevitably be lost."—*Latin Grammar of Andrews and Stoddard*, p. vi. N. Butler, who bestows upon this subject about a dozen duodecimo pages, says in his preface, "The rules for the analysis of sentences, which is a *very useful and interesting* exercise, have been taken from Andrews' and Stoddard's Latin Grammar, some changes and additions being made."—*Butler's Practical Gram.*, p. iv.[332]

OBS. 5.—Wells, in the early copies of his School Grammar, as has been hinted, adopted a method of analysis similar to the *Second* one prescribed above; yet referred, even from the first, to "Andrews and Stoddard's Latin Grammar," and to "De Sacy's General Grammar," as if these were authorities for what he then inculcated. Subsequently, *he changed his scheme*, from that of *Parts Principal* and *Adjuncts*, to one of *Subjects* and *Predicates*, "either grammatical or logical," also "either simple or compound;"—to one resembling Andrews and Stoddard's, yet differing from it, often, as to what constitutes a "grammatical predicate;"—to one resenbling [sic—KTH] the *Third Method* above, yet differing from it, (as does Andrews and Stoddard's,) in taking the logical subject and predicate before the grammatical. "The chapter on Analysis," said he then, "has been Revised and enlarged with great care, and will be found to embody all the most important principles on this subject [.] *which* are contained in the works of De Sacy, Andrews and Stoddard, Kühner, Crosby, and Crane. It is gratifying to observe that the attention of teachers is now so generally directed *to this important mode* of investigating the structure of our language, *in connection with* the ordinary exercises of *etymological* and syntactical parsing."—*Wells's School Gram.*, New Ed., 1850, p. iv.

OBS. 6.—In view of the fact, that Wells's chief mode of sentential analysis had just undergone an almost total metamorphosis, a change plausible perhaps, but of doubtful utility,—that, up to the date of the words just cited, and afterwards, so far and so long as any copies of his early "Thousands" remain in use, the author himself has earnestly directed attention to a method which he now means henceforth to abandon,—in this view, the praise and gratulation expressed above seem singular. If it has been found practicable, to slide "the attention of teachers," and their approbation too, adroitly over from one "important mode of investigating the structure of our language," to an other;—if "it is gratifying to observe," that the direction thus given to public opinion sustains itself so well, and "is so generally" acquiesced in;—if it is proved, that the stereotyped praise of one system of analysis may, without alteration, be so transferred to an other, as to answer the double purpose of commending and superseding;—it is not improbable that the author's next new plates will bear the stamp of yet *other* "most important principles" of analysis. This process is here recommended to be used "*in connection with* the ordinary exercises of *etymological* and syntactical parsing,"—exercises, which, in Wells's Grammar, are generally, and very improperly, commingled; and if, to these, may be profitably conjoined either his present or his former scheme of analysis, it were well, had he somewhere put them together and shown how.

OBS. 7.—But there are other passages of the School Grammar, so little suited to this notion of "*connection*" that one can hardly believe the word ought to be taken in what seems its only sense. "Advanced classes should attend less to the common *Order of Parsing,* and more to the *Analysis* of language."—*Wells's Grammar,* "3d Thousand," p. 125; "113th Thousand," p. 132. This implies, what is probably true of the etymological exercise, that parsing is more rudimental than the other forms of analysis. It also intimates, what is not so clear, that pupils rightly instructed must advance from the former to the latter, as to something more worthy of their intellectual powers. The passage is used with reference to either form of analysis adopted by the author. So the following comparison, in which Parsing is plainly disparaged, stands permanently at the head of "the chapter on Analysis," to commend first one mode, and then an other: "It is particularly desirable that pupils *should pass as early as practicable from the formalities* of common PARSING, to the *more important* exercise of ANALYZING critically the structure of language. The mechanical routine of technical parsing is peculiarly liable to become monotonous and dull, while the *practice of explaining the various relations and offices of words in a sentence,* is adapted to call the mind of the learner into constant and vigorous action, and can hardly fail of exciting the deepest interest,"—*Wells's Gram.*, 3d Th., p. 181; 113th Th., p. 184.

OBS. 8.—An ill scheme of *parsing,* or an ill use of a good one, is almost as unlucky in grammar, as an ill method of *ciphering,* or an ill use of a good one, would be in arithmetic. From the strong contrast cited above, one might suspect that, in selecting, devising, or using, a technical process for the exercising of learners in the principles of etymology and syntax, this author had been less fortunate than the generality of his fellows. Not only is it implied, that parsing is no critical analysis, but even what is set *in opposition* to the "mechanical routine," may very well serve for *a definition* of Syntactical Parsing—"*the practice of explaining the various relations and offices of words in a sentence*!" If this "practice," well ordered, can be at once interesting and profitable to the learner, so may parsing. Nor, after all, is even this author's mode of parsing, defective though it is in several respects, less "important" to the users of his book, or less valued by teachers, than the analysis which he sets above it.

OBS. 9.—S. S. Greene, a public teacher in Boston, who, in answer to a supposed "demand for a *more philosophical plan* of teaching the English language," has entered in earnest upon the "Analysis of Sentences," having devoted to one method of it more than the space of two hundred duodecimo pages, speaks of analysis and of parsing, thus: "The resolving of a sentence into its elements, or of any complex element into the parts which compose it, is called *analysis*."—*Greene's Analysis*, p. 14. "Parsing consists in naming a part of speech, giving its modifications, relation, agreement or dependence, and the rule for its construction. *Analysis* consists in pointing out the words or groups of words which constitute the elements of a sentence. Analysis *should precede* parsing."—*Ib.*, p. 26. "A large proportion of the elements of sentences are not single words, but combinations or groups of words. These groups perform the office of the *substantive,* the *adjective*, or the *adverb,* and, in some one of these relations, enter in as the component parts of a sentence. The pupil who learns to determine the elements of a sentence, *must, therefore, learn the force of these combinations before* he separates them into the single words which compose them. *This advantage* is wholly lost in the ordinary methods of parsing."—*Ib.*, p. 3.

OBS. 10.—On these passages, it may be remarked in the first place, that the distinction attempted between analysis and parsing is by no means clear, or well drawn. Nor indeed could it be; because parsing is a species of analysis. The first assertion would be just as true as it is now, were the former word substituted for the latter: thus, "The resolving of a sentence into its elements, or of any complex element into the *parts* which compose it, is called *parsing*." Next, the "*Parsing*" spoken of in the second sentence, is *Syntactical* Parsing only; and, without a limitation of the species, neither this assertion nor the one concerning precedence is sufficiently true. Again, the suggestion, that, "*Analysis* consists in *pointing out* the words or groups of words which *constitute the elements* of a sentence," has nothing distinctive in it; and, without some idea of the author's peculiar system of "elements," previously impressed upon the mind, is scarcely, if at all, intelligible. Lastly, that a pupil must *understand* a sentence,—or, what is the same thing, "*learn the force of the words combined*,"—before he can be sure of parsing each word rightly, is a very plain and certain truth; but what "advantage" over parsing this truth gives to the lesser analysis, which deals with "groups," it is not easy to discover. If the author had any clear idea of "*this advantage*," he has conveyed no such conception to his readers.

OBS. 11.—Greene's Analysis is the most expanded form of the Third Method above.[333] Its nucleus, or germinating kernel, was the old partition of *subject* and *predicate,* derived from the art of logic. Its chief principles may be briefly stated thus: Sentences, which are simple, or complex, or compound, are made up of *words, phrases,* and *clauses*—three grand classes of elements, called the *first,* the *second,* and the *third* class. From these, each sentence must have two elements; the *Subject,* or Substantive element, and the *Predicate,* or Predicative element, which are principal; and a sentence *may* have five, the subordinates being the Adjective element, the Objective element, and the Adverbial element. The five elements have sundry modifications and subdivisions. Each of the five may, like a sentence, be simple, or complex, or compound; and each may be of any of the three grand classes. The development of this scheme forms a volume, not small. The system is plausible, ingenious, methodical, mostly true, and somewhat elaborate; but it is neither very useful nor very accurate. It seems too much like a great tree, beautiful, symmetrical, and full of leaves, but raised or desired only for fruit, yet bearing little, and some of that little not of good quality, but knurly or bitter. The chief end of a grammar, designed for our tongue, is, to show what is, and what is not, good English. To this end, the system in question does not appear to be well adapted.

OBS. 12.—Dr. Bullions, the projector of the "Series of Grammars, English, Latin, and Greek, all *on the same plan*," inserted in his Latin Grammar, of 1841, a short sketch of the new analysis by "subjects and predicates," "grammatical and logical," the scheme used by Andrews and Stoddard; but his English Grammar, which appeared in 1834, was too early for this "new and improved method of investigating" language. In his later English Grammar, of 1849, however, paying little regard to *sameness of "plan"* or conformity of definitions, he carefully devoted to this matter the space of fifteen pages, placing the topic, not injudiciously, in the first part of his syntax, and referring to it thus in his Preface: "The subject of ANALYSIS, wholly omitted in the former work, is here introduced in its proper place; and to an extent in accordance with its importance."—*Bullions, Analyt. and Pract. Gram.*, p. 3.

OBS. 13.—In applying any of the different methods of analysis, as a school exercise, it will in general perhaps be best to use each *separately*; the teacher directing which one is to be applied, and to what examples. The selections prepared for the stated praxes of this work, will be found as suitable as any. Analysis of sentences is a central and essential matter in the teaching or the study of grammar; but the truest and the most important of the sentential analyses is *parsing*; which, because it is a method distinguished by a technical name of its own, is not commonly denominated analysis. The relation which other methods should bear to *parsing*, is, as we have seen, variously stated by different authors. *Etymological* parsing and *Syntactical* are, or ought to be, distinct exercises. The former, being the most simple, the most elementary, and also requisite to be used before the pupil is prepared for the latter, should, without doubt, take precedence of all the rest, and be made familiar in the first place. Those who say, "*Analysis should precede parsing,*" will scarcely find the application of other analysis practicable, till this is somewhat known. But *Syntactical Parsing* being, when complete in form, the most thorough process of grammatical resolution, it seems proper to have introduced the other methods before it, as above. It can hardly be said that any of these are *necessary* to this exercise, or to one an other; yet in a full course of grammatical instruction, each may at times be usefully employed.

OBS. 14.—Dr. Bullions suggests, that, "*Analysis* should precede *Syntactical parsing*, because, till we know the parts and elements of a sentence, we can not understand their relations, nor intelligently combine them into one consistent whole."—*Analytical and Pract. Gram.*, p. 114. This reason is entirely fictitious and truthless; for the *words* of a sentence are intuitively known to be its "parts and elements;" and, to "*understand* their relations," is as necessary to one form of analysis as to another; but, "intelligently to *combine* them," is no part of the parser's duty: this belongs to the *writer*; and where he has not done it, he must be criticised and censured, as one that knows not well what he says. In W. Allen's Grammar, as in Wells's, Syntactical parsing and Etymological are not divided. Wells intersperses his "Exercises in Parsing," at seven points of his Syntax, and places "the chapter on Analysis," at the end of it. Allen treats first of the several parts of grammar, didactically; then presents a series of exercises adapted to the various heads of the whole. At the beginning of these, are fourteen "Methods of Parsing," which show, successively, the properties and construction of his nine parts of speech; and, *at the ninth method*, which resolves *infinitives*, it is proposed that the pupil begin to apply a method of analysis similar to the Second one above.

EXAMPLES FOR PARSING. PRAXIS XII.—SYNTACTICAL.

_The grand clew to all syntactical parsing is THE SENSE; and as any composition is faulty which does not rightly deliver the authors meaning, so every solution of a word or sentence is necessarily erroneous, in which that meaning is not carefully noticed and literally preserved.

In all complete syntactical parsing, it is required of the pupil—to distinguish the different parts of speech and their classes; to mention their modifications in order; to point out their relation, agreement, or government; and to apply the Rules of Syntax. Thus_:—

EXAMPLE PARSED.

"A young man studious to know his duty, and honestly bent on doing it, will find himself led away from the sin or folly in which the multitude thoughtlessly indulge themselves; but, ah! poor fallen human nature! what conflicts are thy portion, when inclination and habit—a rebel and a traitor—exert their sway against our only saving principle!"—*G. Brown.*

A is the indefinite article: and relates to *man*, or *young man*; according to Rule 1st, which says, "Articles relate to the nouns which they limit." Because the meaning is—*a man—a young man.*

Young is a common adjective, of the positive degree, compared regularly, *young, younger, youngest*: and relates to *man*; according to Rule 9th, which says, "Adjectives relate to nouns or pronouns." Because the meaning is—*young man.*

Man is a common noun, of the third person, singular number, masculine gender, and nominative case: and is the subject of *will find*; according to Rule 2d, which says, "A noun or a pronoun which is the subject of a finite verb, must be in the nominative case." Because the meaning is—*man will find.*

Studious is a common adjective, compared by means of the adverbs; *studious, more studious, most studious*; or, *studious, less studious, least studious*: and relates to *man*; according to Rule 9th, which says, "Adjectives relate to nouns or pronouns." Because the meaning is—*man studious.*

To is a preposition: and shows the relation between *studious* and *know*; according to Rule 23d, which says, "Prepositions show the relations of words, and of the things or thoughts expressed by them." Because the meaning is—*studious to know.*

Know is an irregular active-transitive verb, from *know, knew, knowing, known*; found in the infinitive mood, present tense—no person, or number: and is governed by *to*; according to Rule 18th, which says, "The infinitive mood is governed in general by the preposition TO, which commonly connects it to a finite verb." Because the meaning is—*to know.*

His is a personal pronoun, representing *man*, in the third person, singular number, and masculine gender; according to Rule 10th, which says, "A pronoun must agree with its antecedent, or the noun or pronoun which it represents, in person, number, and gender:" and is in the possessive case, being governed by *duty*; according to Rule 4th, which says, "A noun or a pronoun in the possessive case, is governed by the name of the thing possessed." Because the meaning is—*his duty*;—i. e., the young *man's duty*.

Duty is a common noun, of the third person, singular number, neuter gender, and objective case: and is governed by *know*; according to Rule 5th, which says, "A noun or a pronoun made the object of an active-transitive verb or participle, is governed by it in the objective case." Because the meaning is—to *know* his *duty*.

And is a copulative conjunction: and connects the phrase which follows it, to that which precedes; according to Rule 22d, which says, "Conjunctions connect words, sentences, or parts of sentences." Because the meaning is—studious to know his duty, *and* honestly bent, &c.

Honestly is an adverb of manner: and relates to *bent*; according to Rule 21st, which says, "Adverbs relate to verbs, participles, adjectives, or other adverbs." Because the meaning is—*honestly bent*.

Bent is a perfect participle, from the redundant active-transitive verb, *bend, bent* or *bended, bending, bent* or *bended*: and relates to *man*; according to Rule 20th, which says, "Participles relate to nouns or pronouns, or else are governed by prepositions." Because the meaning is—*man bent*. *On* is a preposition: and shows the relation between *bent* and *doing*; according to Rule 23d, which says, "Prepositions show the relations of words, and of the things or thoughts expressed by them." Because the meaning is—*bent on doing*.

Doing is an imperfect participle, from the irregular active-transitive verb, *do, did, doing, done*: and is governed by on; according to Rule 20th, which says, "Participles relate to nouns or pronouns, or else are governed by prepositions." Because the meaning is—*on doing*.

It is a personal pronoun, representing *duty*, in the third person, singular number, and neuter gender; according to Rule 10th, which says, "A pronoun must agree with its antecedent, or the noun or pronoun which it represents, in person, number, and gender:" and is in the objective case, being governed by *doing*; according to Rule 5th, which says, "A noun or a pronoun made the object of an active-transitive verb or participle, is governed by it in the objective case." Because the meaning is—*doing it*;—i. e., doing *his duty*.

Will find is an irregular active-transitive verb, from *find, found, finding, found*; found in the indicative mood, first-future tense, third person, and singular number: and agrees with its nominative *man*; according to Rule 14th, which says, "Every finite verb must agree with its subject, or nominative, in person and number." Because the meaning is—*man will find*.

Himself is a compound personal pronoun, representing man, in the third person, singular number, and masculine gender; according to Rule 10th, which says, "A pronoun must agree with its antecedent, or the noun or pronoun which it represents, in person, number, and gender;" and is in the objective case, being governed by *will find*; according to Rule 5th, which says, "A noun or a pronoun made the object of an active-transitive verb or participle, is governed by it in the objective case." Because the meaning is—*will find himself*;—i. e., his own mind or person.

Led is a perfect participle, from the irregular active-transitive verb, *lead, led, leading, led*: and relates to *himself*; according to Rule 20th, which says, "Participles relate to nouns or pronouns, or else are governed by prepositions." Because the meaning is—*himself led*.

Away is an adverb of place: and relates to *led*; according to Rule 21st, which says, "Adverbs relate to verbs, participles, adjectives, or other adverbs." Because the meaning is—*led away*.

From is a preposition: and shows the relation between *led* and *sin or folly*; according to Rule 23d, which says, "Prepositions show the relations of words, and of the things or thoughts expressed by them." Because the meaning is—*led from sin or folly*.

The is the definite article: and relates to *sin* and *folly*; according to Rule 1st, which says, "Articles relate to the nouns which they limit." Because the meaning is—*the sin or folly*.

Sin is a common noun, of the third person, singular number, neuter gender, and objective case: and is governed by *from*; according to Rule 7th, which says, "A noun or a pronoun made the object of a preposition, is governed by it in the objective case." Because the meaning is—*from sin*.

Or is a disjunctive conjunction: and connects *sin* and *folly*; according to Rule 22d, which says, "Conjunctions connect words, sentences, or parts of sentences." Because the meaning is—*sin or folly*.

Folly is a common noun, of the third person, singular number, neuter gender, and objective case; and is connected by *or* to *sin*, and governed by the same preposition *from*; according to Rule 7th, which says, "A noun or a pronoun made the object of a preposition, is governed by it in the objective case." Because the meaning is—*from sin or folly*.

In is a preposition: and shows the relation between *indulge* and *which*; according to Rule 23d, which says, "Prepositions show the relations of words, and of the things or thoughts expressed by them." Because the meaning is—*indulge in which*—or, *which they indulge in*.

Which is a relative pronoun, representing *sin or folly*, in the third person, singular number, and neuter gender; according to Rule 13th, which says, "When a pronoun has two or more antecedents connected by *or* or *nor*, it must agree with them singly, and not as if taken together:" and is in the objective case, being governed by *in*; according to Rule 7th, which says, "A noun or a pronoun made the object of a preposition, is governed by it in the objective case." Because the meaning is—*in which*;—i. e., *in which sin or folly*.

The is the definite article: and relates to *multitude*; according to Rule 1st, which says, "Articles relate to the nouns which they limit." Because the meaning is—*the multitude*.

Multitude is a common noun, collective, of the third person, conveying the idea of plurality, masculine gender, and nominative case: and is the subject of *indulge*; according to Rule 2d, which says, "A noun or a pronoun which is the subject of a finite verb, must be in the nominative case." Because the meaning is—*multitude indulge*.

Thoughtlessly is an adverb of manner: and relates to *indulge*; according to Rule 21st, which says, "Adverbs relate to verbs, participles, adjectives, or other adverbs." Because the meaning is—*thoughtlessly indulge*.

Indulge is a regular active-transitive verb, from *indulge, indulged, indulging, indulged*; found in the indicative mood, present tense, third person, and plural number: and agrees with its nominative multitude; according to Rule 15th, which says, "When the nominative is a collective noun conveying the idea of plurality, the verb must agree with it in the plural number." Because the meaning is—*multitude indulge*.

Themselves is a compound personal pronoun, representing *multitude*, in the third person, plural number, and masculine gender; according to Rule 11th, which says, "When the antecedent is a collective noun conveying the idea of plurality, the pronoun must agree with it in the plural number:" and is in the objective case, being governed by *indulge*; according to Rule 5th, which says, "A noun or a pronoun made the object of an active-transitive verb or participle, is governed by it in the objective case." Because the meaning is—*indulge themselves*;—i. e., the individuals of the multitude indulge themselves.

But is a disjunctive conjunction: and connects what precedes and what follows; according to Rule 22d, which says, "Conjunctions connect words, sentences, or parts of sentences." Because the meaning is—A young man, &c., *but*, ah! &c.

Ah is an interjection, indicating sorrow: and is used independently; according to Rule 24th, which says, "Interjections have no dependent construction; they are put absolute, either alone, or with other words." Because the meaning is—*ah!*—unconnected with the rest of the sentence.

Poor is a common adjective, of the positive degree, compared regularly, *poor, poorer, poorest*: and relates to *nature*; according to Rule 9th, which says, "Adjectives relate to nouns or pronouns." Because the meaning is—*poor human nature.*

Fallen is a participial adjective, compared (perhaps) by adverbs: and relates to *nature*; according to Rule 9th, which says, "Adjectives relate to nouns or pronouns." Because the meaning is—*fallen nature.*

Human is a common adjective, not compared: and relates to *nature*; according to Rule 9th, which says, "Adjectives relate to nouns or pronouns." Because the meaning is—*human nature.*

Nature is a common noun, of the second person, singular number, neuter gender, and nominative case: and is put absolute by direct address; according to Rule 8th, which says, "A noun or a pronoun is put absolute in the nominative, when its case depends on no other word." Because the meaning is—*poor fallen human nature!*—the noun being unconnected with any verb.

What is a pronominal adjective, not compared: and relates to *conflicts*; according to Rule 9th, which says, "Adjectives relate to nouns or pronouns." Because the meaning is—*what conflicts.*

Conflicts is a common noun, of the third person, plural number, neuter gender, and nominative case: and is the subject of *are*; according to Rule 2d, which says, "A noun or a pronoun which is the subject of a finite verb, must be in the nominative case." Because the meaning is—*conflicts are.*

Are is an irregular neuter verb, from *be, was, being, been*; found in the indicative mood, present tense, third person, and plural number: and agrees with its nominative *conflicts*; according to Rule 14th, which says, "Every finite verb must agree with its subject, or nominative, in person and number." Because the meaning is—*conflicts are.*

Thy is a personal pronoun, representing *nature*, in the second person, singular number, and neuter gender; according to Rule 10th, which says, "A pronoun must agree with its antecedent, or the noun or pronoun which it represents, in person, number, and gender:" and is in the possessive case, being governed by *portion*; according to Rule 4th, which says, "A noun or a pronoun in the possessive case, is governed by the name of the thing possessed." Because the meaning is—*thy portion.*

Portion is a common noun, of the third person, singular number, neuter gender, and nominative case: and is put after *are,* in agreement with *conflicts*; according to Rule 6th, which says, "A noun or a pronoun put after a verb or participle not transitive, agrees in case with a preceding noun or pronoun referring to the same thing." Because the meaning is—*conflicts are thy portion.*

When is a conjunctive adverb of time: and relates to the two verbs, *are* and *exert*; according to Rule 21st, which says, "Adverbs relate to verbs, participles, adjectives, or other adverbs." Because the meaning is—what conflicts *are* thy portion, *when* inclination and habit *exert*, &c.

Inclination is a common noun, of the third person, singular number, neuter gender, and nominative case: and is one of the subjects of *exert*; according to Rule 2d, which says, "A noun or a pronoun which is the subject of a finite verb, must be in the nominative case." Because the meaning is—*inclination and habit exert*.

And is a copulative conjunction: and connects *inclination* and *habit*; according to Rule 22d, which says, "Conjunctions connect words, sentences, or parts of sentences." Because the meaning is—*inclination and habit*.

Habit is a common noun, of the third person, singular number, neuter gender, and nominative case: and is one of the subjects of *exert*; according to Rule 2d, which says, "A noun or a pronoun which is the subject of a finite verb, must be in the nominative case." Because the meaning is—*inclination and habit exert*.

A is the indefinite article: and relates to *rebel*; according to Rule 1st, which says, "Articles relate to the nouns which they limit." Because the meaning is—*a rebel*.

Rebel is a common noun, of the third person, singular number, masculine gender, and nominative case: and is put in apposition with *inclination*; according to Rule 3d, which says, "A noun or a personal pronoun used to explain a preceding noun or pronoun, is put, by apposition, in the same case." Because the meaning is—*inclination, a rebel*.

And is a copulative conjunction: and connects *rebel* and *traitor*; according to Rule 22d, which says, "Conjunctions connect words, sentences, or parts of sentences." Because the meaning is—*a rebel and a traitor*.

A is the indefinite article: and relates to *traitor*; according to Rule 1st, which says, "Articles relate to the nouns which they limit." Because the meaning is—*a traitor*.

Traitor is a common noun, of the third person, singular number, masculine gender, and nominative case: and is put in apposition with *habit*; according to Rule 3d, which says, "A noun or a personal pronoun used to explain a preceding noun or pronoun, is put, by apposition, in the same case." Because the meaning is—*habit, a traitor*.

Exert is a regular active-transitive verb, from *exert, exerted, exerting, exerted*; found in the indicative mood, present tense, third person, and plural number: and agrees with its two nominatives *inclination and habit*; according to Rule 16th, which says, "When a verb has two or more nominatives connected by *and*, it must agree with them jointly in the plural, because they are taken together." Because the meaning is—*inclination and habit exert*.

Their is a personal pronoun, representing *inclination and habit*, in the third person, plural number, and neuter gender; according to Rule 12th, which says, "When a pronoun has two or more antecedents connected by *and*, it must agree with them jointly in the plural, because they are taken together:" and is in the possessive case, being governed by *sway*; according to Rule 4th, which says, "A noun or a pronoun in the possessive case, is governed by the name of the thing possessed." Because the meaning is—*their sway*;—i. e., the sway of inclination and habit.

Sway is a common noun, of the third person, singular number, neuter gender, and objective case; and is governed by *exert*; according to Rule 5th, which says, "A noun or a pronoun made the object of an active-transitive verb or participle, is governed by it in the objective case." Because the meaning is—*exert sway*.

Against is a preposition: and shows the relation between *exert* and *principle*; according to Rule 23d, which says, "Prepositions show the relations of words, and of the things or thoughts expressed by them." Because the meaning is—*exert against principle*.

Our is a personal pronoun, representing *the speakers*, in the first person, plural number, and masculine gender; according to Rule 10th, which says, "A pronoun must agree with its antecedent, or the noun or pronoun which it represents, in person, number, and gender:" and is in the possessive case, being governed by *principle*; according to Rule 4th, which says, "A noun or a pronoun in the possessive case, is governed by the name of the thing possessed." Because the meaning is—*our principle*;—i. e., the *speakers*' principle.

Only is a pronominal adjective, not compared: and relates to *principle*; according to Rule 9th, which says, "Adjectives relate to nouns or pronouns." Because the meaning is—*only principle*.

Saving is a participial adjective, compared by adverbs when it means *frugal*, but not compared in the sense here intended: and relates to *principle*; according to Rule 9th, which says, "Adjectives relate to nouns or pronouns." Because the meaning is—*saving principle*.

Principle is a common noun, of the third person, singular number, neuter gender, and objective case: and is governed by *against*; according to Rule 7th, which says, "A noun or a pronoun made the object of a preposition, is governed by it in the objective case." Because the meaning is—*against principle.*

LESSON I.—ARTICLES.

"In English heroic verse, the capital pause of every line, is determined by the sense to be after the fourth, the fifth, the sixth or the seventh syllable."—*Kames, El. of Crit.*, ii, 105.

"When, in considering the structure of a tree or a plant, we observe how all the parts, the roots, the stem, the bark, and the leaves, are suited to the growth and nutriment of the whole; when we survey all the parts and members of a living animal; or when we examine any of the curious works of art—such as a clock, a ship, or any nice machine; the pleasure which we have in the survey, is wholly founded on this sense of beauty."—*Blair's Rhet.*, p. 49.

"It never can proceed from a good taste, to make a teaspoon resemble the leaf of a tree; for such a form is inconsistent with the destination of a teaspoon."—*Kames, El. of Crit.*, ii, 351.

"In an epic poem, a history, an oration, or any work of genius, we always require a fitness, or an adjustment of means to the end which the author is supposed to have in view."—*Blair's Rhet.*, p. 50.

"Rhetoric, Logic, and Grammar, are three arts that should always walk hand in hand. The first is the art of speaking eloquently; the second, that of thinking well; and the third, that of speaking with propriety."—*Formey's Belles-Lettres*, p. 114.

"Spring hangs her infant blossoms on the trees,
Rock'd in the cradle of the western breeze."—*Cowper.*

LESSON II.—NOUNS.

"There goes a rumour that I am to be banished. And let the sentence come, if God so will. The other side of the sea is my Father's ground, as well as this side."—*Rutherford*.

"Gentlemen, there is something on earth greater than arbitrary or despotic power. The lightning has its power, and the whirlwind has its power, and the earthquake has its power. But there is something among men more capable of shaking despotic power than lightning, whirlwind, or earthquake; that is—the threatened indignation of the whole civilized world."—*Daniel Webster*.

"And Isaac sent away Jacob; and he went to Padan Aram, unto Laban, son of Bethuel the Syrian, and brother of Rebecca, Jacob's and Esau's mother."—See *Gen.*, xxviii, 5.

"The purpose you undertake is dangerous." "Why that is certain: it is dangerous to take a cold, to sleep, to drink; but I tell you, my Lord fool, out of this nettle danger, we pluck this flower safety."—*Shakespeare*.

"And towards the Jews alone, one of the noblest charters of liberty on earth—*Magna Charta*, the Briton's boast—legalized an act of injustice."—*Keith's Evidences*, p. 74.

"Were Demosthenes's Philippics spoken in a British assembly, in a similar conjuncture of affairs, they would convince and persuade at this day. The rapid style, the vehement reasoning, the disdain, anger, boldness, freedom, which perpetually animate them, would render their success infallible over any modern assembly. I question whether the same can be said of Cicero's orations; whose eloquence, however beautiful, and however well suited to the Roman taste, yet borders oftener on declamation, and is more remote from the manner in which we now expect to hear real business and causes of importance treated."—*Blair's Rhet.*, p. 248.

"In fact, every attempt to present on paper the splendid effects of impassioned eloquence, is like gathering up dewdrops, which appear jewels and pearls on the grass, but run to water in the hand; the essence and the elements remain, but the grace, the sparkle, and the form, are gone."—*Montgomery's Life of Spencer*.

"As in life true dignity must be founded on character, not on dress and appearance; so in language the dignity of composition must arise from sentiment and thought, not from ornament."—*Blair's Rhet.*, p. 144.

"And man, whose heaven-erected face the smiles of love adorn,
Man's inhumanity to man makes countless thousands mourn."
—*Burns*.

"Ah wretched man! unmindful of thy end!
A moment's glory! and what fates attend."
—*Pope, Iliad*, B. xvii, l. 231.

LESSON III.—ADJECTIVES.

"Embarrassed, obscure, and feeble sentences, are generally, if not always, the result of embarrassed, obscure, and feeble thought."—*Blair's Rhet.*, p. 120.

"Upon this ground, we prefer a simple and natural, to an artificial and affected style; a regular and well-connected story, to loose and scattered narratives; a catastrophe which is tender and pathetic, to one which leaves us unmoved."—*Ib.*, p. 23.

"A thorough good taste may well be considered as a power compounded of natural sensibility to beauty, and of improved understanding."—*Ib.*, p. 18.

"Of all writings, ancient or modern, the sacred Scriptures afford us the highest instances of the sublime. The descriptions of the Deity, in them, are wonderfully noble; both from the grandeur of the object, and the manner of representing it."—*Ib.*, p. 36.

"It is not the authority of any one person, or of a few, be they ever so eminent, that can establish one form of speech in preference to another. Nothing but the general practice of good writers and good speakers can do it."—*Priestley's Gram.*, p. 107.

"What other means are there to attract love and esteem so effectual as a virtuous course of life? If a man be just and beneficent, if he be temperate, modest, and prudent, he will infallibly gain the esteem and love of all who know him."—*Kames, El. of Crit.*, i, 167.

"But there are likewise, it must be owned, people in the world, whom it is easy to make worse by rough usage, and not easy to make better by any other."—*Abp. Seeker.*

"The great comprehensive truth written in letters of living light on every page of our history—the language addressed by every past age of New England to all future ages, is this: Human happiness has no perfect security but freedom;—freedom, none but virtue;—virtue, none but knowledge: and neither freedom, nor virtue, nor knowledge, has any vigour or immortal hope, except in the principles of the Christian faith, and in the sanctions of the Christian religion."—*President Quincy.*

"For bliss, as thou hast part, to me is bliss;
Tedious, unshared with thee, and odious soon."
—*P. Lost*, B. ix, l. 880.

LESSON IV.—PRONOUNS.

"There is but one governor whose sight we cannot escape, whose power we cannot resist: a sense of His presence and of duty to Him, will accomplish more than all the laws and penalties which can be devised without it."—*Woodbridge, Lit. C.*, p. 154.

"Every voluntary society must judge who shall be members of their body, and enjoy fellowship with them in their peculiar privileges."—*Watts*.

"Poetry and impassioned eloquence are the only sources from which the living growth of a language springs; and even if in their vehemence they bring down some mountain rubbish along with them, this sinks to the bottom, and the pure stream flows along over it."—*Philological Museum*, i, 645. "This use is bounded by the province, county, or district, which gives name to the dialect, and beyond which its peculiarities are sometimes unintelligible, and always ridiculous."—*Campbell's Rhet.*, p. 163.

"Every thing that happens, is both a cause and an effect; being the effect of what goes before, and the cause of what follows."—*Kames, El. of Crit.*, ii, 297.

"Withhold not good from them to whom it is due, when it is in the power of thine hand to do it."—*Prov.*, iii, 27.

"Yet there is no difficulty at all in ascertaining the idea. * * * By reflecting upon that which is myself now, and that which was myself twenty years ago, I discern they are not two, but one and the same self."—*Butler's Analogy*, p. 271.

"If you will replace what has been long expunged from the language, and extirpate what is firmly rooted, undoubtedly you yourself become an innovator."—*Campbell's Rhet.*, p. 167; *Murray's Gram.*, 364.

"To speak as others speak, is one of those tacit obligations, annexed to the condition of living in society, which we are bound in conscience to fulfill, though we have never ratified them by any express promise; because, if they were disregarded, society would be impossible, and human happiness at an end."—See *Murray's Gram.*, 8vo, p. 139.

"In England *thou* was in current use until, perhaps, near the commencement of the seventeenth century, though it was getting to be regarded as somewhat disrespectful. At Walter Raleigh's trial, Coke, when argument and evidence failed him, insulted the defendant by applying to him the term *thou*. 'All that Lord Cobham did,' he cried, 'was at *thy* instigation, *thou* viper! for I *thou* thee, *thou* traitor!'"—*Fowler's E. Gram.*, §220.

"Th' Egyptian crown I to your hands remit;
And with it take his heart who offers it."—*Shakspeare*.

LESSON V.—VERBS.

"Sensuality contaminates the body, depresses the understanding, deadens the moral feelings of the heart, and degrades man from his rank in the creation."—*Murray's Key*, ii, p. 231.

"When a writer reasons, we look only for perspicuity; when he describes, we expect embellishment; when he divides, or relates, we desire plainness and simplicity."—*Blair's Rhet.*, p. 144.

"Livy and Herodotus are diffuse; Thucydides and Sallust are succinct; yet all of them are agreeable."—*Ib.*, p. 178.

"Whenever petulant ignorance, pride, malice, malignity, or envy, interposes to cloud or sully his fame, I will take upon me to pronounce that the eclipse will not last long."—*Dr. Delany.*

"She said she had nothing to say, for she was resigned, and I knew all she knew that concerned us in this world; but she desired to be alone, that in the presence of God only, she might without interruption do her last duty to me."—*Spect.*, No. 520.

"Wisdom and truth, the offspring of the sky, are immortal; while cunning and deception, the meteors of the earth, after glittering for a moment, must pass away."—*Robert Hall.* "See, I have this day set thee over the nations, and over the kingdoms, to root out, and to pull down, and to destroy, and to throw down, to build, and to plant."—*Jeremiah*, i, 10.

"God might command the stones to be made bread, or the clouds to rain it; but he chooses rather to leave mankind to till, to sow, to reap, to gather into barns, to grind, to knead, to bake, and then to eat."—*London Quarterly Review.*

"Eloquence is no invention of the schools. Nature teaches every man to be eloquent, when he is much in earnest. Place him in some critical situation, let him have some great interest at stake, and you will see him lay hold of the most effectual means of persuasion."—*Blair's Rhet.*, p. 235.

"It is difficult to possess great fame and great ease at the same time. Fame, like fire, is with difficulty kindled, is easily increased, but dies away if not continually fed. To preserve fame alive, every enterprise ought to be a pledge of others, so as to keep mankind in constant expectation."—*Art of Thinking*, p. 50. "Pope, finding little advantage from external help, resolved thenceforward to direct himself, and at twelve formed a plan of study which he completed with little other incitement than the desire of excellence."—*Johnson's Lives of Poets*, p. 498.

"Loose, then, from earth the grasp of fond desire,
Weigh anchor, and some happier clime explore."—*Young*.

LESSON VI.—PARTICIPLES.

"The child, affrighted with the view of his father's helmet and crest, and clinging to the nurse; Hector, putting off his helmet, taking the child into his arms, and offering up a prayer for him; Andromache, receiving back the child with a smile of pleasure, and at the same instant bursting into tears; form the most natural and affecting picture that can possibly be imagined."—*Blair's Rhet.*, p. 435.

"The truth of being, and the truth of knowing are one; differing no more than the direct beam and the beam reflected."—*Ld. Bacon*. "Verbs denote states of being, considered as beginning, continuing, ending, being renewed, destroyed, and again repeated, so as to suit any occasion."—*William Ward's Gram.*, p. 41.

"We take it for granted, that we have a competent knowledge and skill, and that we are able to acquit ourselves properly, in our own native tongue; a faculty, solely acquired by use, conducted by habit, and tried by the ear, carries us on without reflection."—*Lowth's Gram.*, p. vi.

"I mean the teacher himself; who, stunned with the hum, and suffocated with the closeness of his school-room, has spent the whole day in controlling petulance, exciting indifference to action, striving to enlighten stupidity, and labouring to soften obstinacy."—*Sir W. Scott.*

"The inquisitive mind, beginning with criticism, the most agreeable of all amusements, and finding no obstruction in its progress, advances far into the sensitive part of our nature; and gains imperceptibly a thorough knowledge of the human heart, of its desires, and of every motive to action."—*Kames, El. of Crit.*, i, 42.

"They please, are pleased; they give to get esteem;
Till, seeming blest, they grow to what they seem."—*Goldsmith.*

LESSON VII.—ADVERBS.

"How cheerfully, how freely, how regularly, how constantly, how unweariedly, how powerfully, how extensively, he communicateth his convincing, his enlightening, his heart-penetrating, warming, and melting; his soul-quickening, healing, refreshing, directing, and fructifying influence!"—*Brown's Metaphors*, p. 96.

"The passage, I grant, requires to be well and naturally read, in order to be promptly comprehended; but surely there are very few passages worth comprehending, either of verse or prose, that can be promptly understood, when they are read unnaturally and ill."—*Thelwall's Lect.* "They waste life in what are called good resolutions—partial efforts at reformation, feebly commenced, heartlessly conducted, and hopelessly concluded."—*Maturin's Sermons*, p. 262.

"A man may, in respect of grammatical purity, speak unexceptionably, and yet speak obscurely and ambiguously; and though we cannot say, that a man may speak properly, and at the same time speak unintelligibly, yet this last case falls more naturally to be considered as an offence against perspicuity, than as a violation of propriety."—*Jamieson's Rhet.*, p. 104.

"Ye are witnesses, and God also, how holily and justly and unblamably we behaved ourselves among you that believe."—*1 Thes.*, ii, 10.

"The question is not, whether they know what is said of Christ in the Scriptures; but whether they know it savingly, truly, livingly, powerfully."—*Penington's Works*, iii, 28.

"How gladly would the man recall to life
The boy's neglected sire! a mother too,
That softer friend, perhaps more gladly still,
Might he demand them at the gates of death!"—*Cowper.*

LESSON VIII.—CONJUNCTIONS.

"Every person's safety requires that he should submit to be governed; for if one man may do harm without suffering punishment, every man has the same right, and no person can be safe."—*Webster's Essays*, p. 38.

"When it becomes a practice to collect debts by law, it is a proof of corruption and degeneracy among the people. Laws and courts are necessary, to settle controverted points between man and man; but a man should pay an acknowledged debt, not because there is a law to oblige him, but because it is just and honest, and because he has promised to pay it."—*Ib.*, p. 42.

"The liar, and only the liar, is invariably and universally despised, abandoned, and disowned. It is therefore natural to expect, that a crime thus generally detested, should be generally avoided."—*Hawkesworth*.

"When a man swears to the truth of his tale, he tacitly acknowledges that his bare word does not deserve credit. A swearer will lie, and a liar is not to be believed even upon his oath; nor is he believed, when he happens to speak the truth."—*Red Book*, p. 108.

"John Adams replied, 'I know Great Britain has determined on her system, and that very determination determines me on mine. You know I have been constant and uniform in opposition to her measures. The die is now cast. I have passed the Rubicon. Sink or swim, live or die, survive or perish with my country, is my unalterable determination.'"—SEWARD'S *Life of John Quincy Adams*, p. 26.

"I returned, and saw under the sun that the race is not to the swift, nor the battle to the strong, neither yet bread to the wise, nor yet riches to men of understanding, nor yet favour to men of skill; but time and chance happen to them all."—*Ecclesiastes*, ix, 11.

"Little, alas! is all the good I can;
A man oppress'd, dependent, yet a man."—*Pope, Odys.*, B. xiv, p. 70.

LESSON IX.—PREPOSITIONS.

"He who legislates only for a party, is engraving his name on the adamantine pillar of his country's history, to be gazed on forever as an object of universal detestation."—*Wayland's Moral Science*, p. 401.

"The Greek language, in the hands of the orator, the poet, and the historian, must be allowed to bear away the palm from every other known in the world; but to that only, in my opinion, need our own yield the precedence."—*Barrow's Essays*, p. 91.

"For my part, I am convinced that the method of teaching which approaches most nearly to the method of investigation, is incomparably the best; since, not content with serving up a few barren and lifeless truths, it leads to the stock on which they grew."—*Burke, on Taste*, p. 37. Better —"on which *truths grow*."

"All that I have done in this difficult part of grammar, concerning the proper use of prepositions, has been to make a few general remarks upon the subject; and then to give a collection of instances, that have occurred to me, of the improper use of some of them."—*Priestley's Gram.*, p. 155.

"This is not an age of encouragement for works of elaborate research and real utility. The genius of the trade of literature is necessarily unfriendly to such productions."—*Thelwall's Lect.*, p. 102.

"At length, at the end of a range of trees, I saw three figures seated on a bank of moss, with a silent brook creeping at their feet."—*Steele*.

"Thou rather, with thy sharp and sulph'rous bolt,
Splitst the unwedgeable and gnarled oak."—*Shakspeare*.

LESSON X.—INTERJECTIONS.

"Hear the word of the Lord, O king of Judah, that sittest upon the throne of David; thou, and thy servants, and thy people, that enter in by these gates: thus saith the Lord, Execute ye judgement and righteousness, and deliver the spoiled out of the hand of the oppressor."—*Jeremiah*, xxii, 2, 3.

"Therefore, thus saith the Lord concerning Jehoiakim the son of Josiah king of Judah, They shall not lament for him, saying, Ah my brother! or, Ah sister! they shall not lament for him, saying, Ah lord! or, Ah his glory! He shall be buried with the burial of an ass, drawn and cast forth beyond the gates of Jerusalem."—*Jer.*, xxii, 18, 19.

"O thou afflicted, tossed with tempest, and not comforted, behold, I will lay thy stones with fair colours, and lay thy foundations with sapphires."—*Isaiah*, liv, 11.

"O prince! O friend! lo! here thy Medon stands;
Ah! stop the hero's unresisted hands."
   —*Pope, Odys.*, B. xxii, l. 417.

"When, lo! descending to our hero's aid,
Jove's daughter Pallas, war's triumphant maid!"
   —*Ib.*, B. xxii, l. 222.

"O friends! oh ever exercised in care!
Hear Heaven's commands, and reverence what ye hear!"
   —*Ib.*, B. xii, l. 324.

"Too daring prince! ah, whither dost thou run?
Ah, too forgetful of thy wife and you!"
   —*Pope's Iliad*, B. vi, l. 510.

CHAPTER II.—ARTICLES.

In this chapter, and those which follow it, the Rules of Syntax are again exhibited, in the order of the parts of speech, with Examples, Exceptions, Observations, Notes, and False Syntax. The Notes are all of them, in form and character, subordinate rules of syntax, designed for the detection of errors. The correction of the False Syntax placed under the rules and notes, will form an *oral exercise*, similar to that of parsing, and perhaps more useful.[334]

RULE I.—ARTICLES.

Articles relate to the nouns which they limit:[335] as, "At *a* little distance from *the* ruins of *the* abbey, stands *an* aged elm."

"See *the* blind beggar dance, *the* cripple sing,
The sot *a* hero, lunatic *a* king."—*Pope's Essay*, Ep. ii, l. 268.

EXCEPTION FIRST.

The definite article used *intensively*, may relate to an *adjective* or *adverb* of the comparative or the superlative degree; as, "A land which was *the mightiest*."—*Byron*. "*The farther* they proceeded, *the greater* appeared their alacrity."—*Dr. Johnson*. "He chooses it *the rather*"—*Cowper*. See Obs. 10th, below.

EXCEPTION SECOND.

The indefinite article is sometimes used to give a collective meaning to what seems a *plural adjective of number*; as, "Thou hast *a few* names even in Sardis."—*Rev.*, iii, 4. "There are *a thousand* things which crowd into my memory."—*Spectator*, No. 468. "The centurion commanded *a hundred* men."—*Webster*. See Etymology, Articles, Obs. 26.

OBSERVATIONS ON RULE I.

OBS. 1.—The article is a kind of *index*, usually pointing to some noun; and it is a general, if not a universal, principle, that no one noun admits of more than one article. Hence, two or more articles in a sentence are signs of two or more nouns; and hence too, by a very convenient ellipsis, an article before an adjective is often made to relate to a noun understood; as, "*The* grave [*people*] rebuke *the* gay [*people*], and *the* gay [*people*] mock *the* grave" [*people*].—*Maturin's Sermons*, p. 103. "*The* wise [*persons*] shall inherit glory."—*Prov.*, iii, 35. "*The* vile [*person*] will talk villainy."—*Coleridge's Lay Sermons,* p. 105: see *Isaiah*, xxxii, 6. "The testimony of the Lord is sure, making wise *the* simple" [*ones*].—*Psal.*, xix, 7. "*The* Old [*Testament*] and the New Testament are alike authentic."—"*The* animal [*world*] and the vegetable world are adapted to each other."—"*An* epic [*poem*] and a dramatic poem are the same in substance."—*Ld. Kames, El. of Crit.*, ii, 274. "The neuter verb is conjugated like *the* active" [*verb*].—*Murray's Gram.*, p. 99. "Each section is supposed to contain *a* heavy [*portion*] and a light portion; *the* heavy [*portion*] being the accented syllable, and *the* light [*portion*] *the* unaccented" [*syllable*].—*Rush, on the Voice*, p. 364.

OBS. 2.—Our language does not, like the French, *require a repetition* of the article before every noun in a series; because the same article may serve to limit the signification of several nouns, provided they all stand in the same construction. Hence the following sentence is bad English: "The understanding and language have a strict connexion."—*Murray's Gram.*, i, p. 356. The sense of the former noun only was meant to be limited. The expression therefore should have been, "*Language and the understanding* have a strict connexion," or, "The understanding *has* a strict connexion *with language.*" In some instances, one article *seems* to limit the sense of several nouns that are not all in the same construction, thus: "As it proves a greater or smaller obstruction to *the speaker's* or *writer's aim.*"—*Campbell's Rhet.*, p. 200. That is—"to *the* aim of *the* speaker or *the* writer." It is, in fact, the possessive, that limits the other nouns; for, "*a man's foes*" means, "*the* foes of *a* man;" and, "*man's wisdom,*" means, "*the* wisdom of man." The governing noun cannot have an article immediately before it. Yet the omission of articles, when it occurs, is not properly *by ellipsis*, as some grammarians declare it to be; for there never can be a proper ellipsis of an article, when there is not also an ellipsis of its noun. Ellipsis supposes the omitted words to be necessary to the construction, when they are not so to the sense; and this, it would seem, cannot be the case with a mere article. If such a sign be in any wise necessary, it ought to be used; and if not needed in any respect, it cannot be said to be *understood*. The definite article being generally required before adjectives that are used by ellipsis as nouns, we in this case repeat it before every term in a series; as, "They are singled out from among their fellows, as *the* kind, *the* amiable, *the* sweet-tempered, *the* upright."—*Dr. Chalmers.*

"*The* great, *the* gay, shall they partake The heav'n that thou alone canst make?"—*Cowper.*

OBS. 3.—The article precedes its noun, and is never, by itself, placed after it; as, "Passion is *the* drunkenness of *the* mind."—*Southey*. When an *adjective* likewise precedes the noun, the article is usually placed before the adjective, that its power of limitation may extend over that also; as, "*A concise* writer compresses his thoughts into *the fewest* possible words."—*Blair's Rhet.*, p. 176.

"*The private* path, *the secret* acts of men, If noble, far *the noblest* of their lives."—*Young.*

OBS. 4.—The relative position of the article and the adjective is seldom a matter of indifference. Thus, it is good English to say, "*both the men*," or, "*the two men;*" but we can by no means say, "*the both men*" or, "*two the men.*" Again, the two phrases, "*half a dollar,*" and "*a half dollar,*" though both good, are by no means equivalent. Of the pronominal adjectives, some exclude the article; some precede it; and some follow it, like other adjectives. The word *same* is seldom, if ever used without the definite article or some stronger definitive before it; as, "On *the same* day,"—"in *that same* hour,"—"*These same* gentlemen." After the adjective *both*, the definite article *may* be used, but it is generally *unnecessary*, and this is a sufficient reason for omitting it: as, "The following sentences will fully exemplify, to the young grammarian, *both the parts* of this rule."—*Murray's Gram.*, i, p. 192. Say, "*both parts.*" The adjective *few* may be used either with or without an article, but not with the same import: as, "*The few* who were present, were in the secret;" i. e., All then present knew the thing. "*Few* that were present, were in the secret;" i.e., Not many then present knew the thing. "When I say, 'There were *few* men with him,' I speak diminutively, and mean to represent them as inconsiderable; whereas, when I say, 'There were *a few* men with him,' I evidently intend to make the most of them."—*Murray's Gram.*, p. 171. See Etymology, Articles, Obs. 28.

OBS. 5.—The pronominal adjectives which exclude the article, are *any, each, either, every, much, neither, no,* or *none, some, this, that, these, those.* The pronominal adjectives which precede the article, are *all, both, many, such*, and *what*; as, "*All the* world,"—"*Both the* judges,"—"*Many a*[336] mile,"—"*Such a* chasm,"—"*What a* freak." In like manner, any adjective of quality, when its meaning is limited by the adverb *too, so, as,* or *how,* is put before the article; as, "*Too great a* study of strength, is found to betray writers into a harsh manner."—*Blair's Rhet.*, p. 179. "Like *many an* other poor wretch, I now suffer *all the* ill consequences of *so foolish an* indulgence." "*Such a* gift is *too small a* reward for *so great a* labour."—*Brightland's Gram.*, p. 95. "Here flows *as clear a* stream as any in Greece. *How beautiful a* prospect is here!"—*Bicknell's Gram.*, Part ii, p. 52. The pronominal adjectives which follow the article, are *few, former, first, latter, last, little, one, other,* and *same*; as, "An author might lean either to *the one* [style] or to *the other*, and yet be beautiful."—*Blair's Rhet.*, p. 179. *Many,* like *few,* sometimes follows the article; as, "*The many* favours which we have received."—"In conversation, for *many a man*, they say, *a many men*."—*Johnson's Dict.* In this order of the words, *a* seems awkward and needless; as,

"Told of *a many* thousand warlike French."—*Shak.*

OBS. 6.—When the adjective is preceded by any other adverb than *too, so, as,* or *how,* the article is almost always placed before the adverb: as, "One of *the* most complete models;"—"*An* equally important question;"—"*An* exceedingly rough passage;"—"*A* very important difference." The adverb *quite,* however, may be placed either before or after the article, though perhaps with a difference of construction: as, "This is *quite a* different thing;"—or, "This is *a quite different* thing." "Finding it *quite an* other thing;"—or, "Finding it *a quite other* thing."—*Locke, on Ed.*, p. 153. Sometimes *two adverbs* intervene between the article and the adjective; as, "We had a *rather more* explicit account of the Novii."—*Philol. Museum,* i, 458. But when an other adverb follows *too, so, as,* or *how,* the three words should be placed either before the article or after the noun; as, "Who stands there in *so purely poetical* a light."—*Ib.*, i, 449. Better, perhaps: "*In a light so purely poetical.*"

OBS. 7.—The definitives *this, that,* and some others, though they supersede the article *an* or *a,* may be followed by the adjective *one*; for we say, "*this one thing,*" but not, "*this a thing.*" Yet, in the following sentence, *this* and *a* being separated by other words, appear to relate to the same noun: "For who is able to judge *this* thy so great *a* people?"—*1 Kings*, iii, 9. But we may suppose the noun *people* to be understood after *this*. Again, the following example, if it is not wrong, has an ellipsis of the word *use* after the first *a*:

"For highest cordials all their virtue lose,
By *a* too frequent and too bold *a* use."—*Pomfret.*

OBS. 8.—When the adjective is placed *after* the noun, the article generally retains its place before the noun, and is not repeated before the adjective: as, "*A* man *ignorant* of astronomy;"—"*The* primrose *pale.*" In *Greek*, when an adjective is placed after its noun, if the article is applied to the noun, it is repeated before the adjective; as, "[Greek: Hæ polis hæ megalæ,]"—"*The* city *the* great;" i.e., "The great city." [337]

OBS. 9.—Articles, according to their own definition and nature, come *before* their nouns; but the definite article and an adjective seem sometimes to be placed after the noun to which they both relate: as, "Section *the Fourth*;"—"Henry *the Eighth*." Such examples, however, may possibly be supposed elliptical; as, "Section, *the fourth division* of the chapter;"—"Henry, *the eighth king* of that name:" and, if they are so, the article, in *English*, can never be placed after its noun, nor can two articles ever properly relate to one noun, in any particular construction of it. Priestley observes, "Some writers affect to *transpose* these words, and place the numeral adjective first; [as,] '*The first Henry.*' Hume's History, Vol. i, p.

497. This construction is common with this writer, but there seems to be a *want of dignity* in it."—*Rudiments of E. Gram.*, p. 150. Dr. Webster cites the word *Great*, in "Alexander the Great" as a *name*, or *part* of a name; that is, he gives it as an instance of "*cognomination.*" See his *American Dict.*, 8vo. And if this is right, the article may be said to relate to the epithet only, as it appears to do. For, if the word is taken substantively, there is certainly no ellipsis; neither is there any transposition in putting it last, but rather, as Priestley suggests, in putting it first.

OBS. 10.—The definite article is often prefixed to *comparatives* and *superlatives*; and its effect is, as Murray observes, (in the words of Lowth,) "to mark the degree *the more* strongly, and to define it *the more* precisely: as, '*The more* I examine it, *the better* I like it.' 'I like this *the least* of any.'"—*Murray's Gram.*, p. 33; *Lowth's*, 14. "For neither if we eat, are we *the better*; neither if we eat not, are we *the worse.*"—*1 Cor.*, viii, 8. "One is not *the more* agreeable to me for loving beef, as I do; nor *the less* agreeable for preferring mutton."—*Kames, El. of Crit.*, Vol. ii, p. 365. "They are not the men in the nation, *the most* difficult to be replaced."—*Priestley's Gram.*, p. 148. In these instances, the article seems to be used *adverbially,* and to relate only to the *adjective* or *adverb* following it. (See observation fourth, on the Etymology of Adverbs.) Yet none of our grammarians have actually reckoned *the* an adverb. After the *adjective*, the noun might perhaps be supplied; but when the word *the* is added to an *adverb*, we must either call it an adverb, or make an exception to Rule 1st above: and if an exception is to be made, the brief form which I have given, cannot well be improved. For even if a noun be understood, it may not appear that the article relates to it, rather than to the degree of the quality. Thus: "*The* deeper the well, *the* clearer the water." This Dr. Ash supposes to mean, "The deeper *well* the well *is*, the clearer *water* the water *is.*"—*Ash's Gram.*, p. 107. But does the text specify a *particular* "deeper well" or "clearer water?" I think not. To what then does *the* refer, but to the proportionate degree of *deeper* and *clearer*?

OBS. 11.—The article the is sometimes elegantly used, after an idiom common in the French language, in lieu of a possessive pronoun; as, "He looked him full in *the* face; i. e. in *his* face."—*Priestley's Gram.*, p. 150. "Men who have not bowed *the knee* to the image of Baal."—*Rom.*, xi, 4. That is, *their knees*.

OBS. 12.—The article *an* or *a*, because it implies unity, is applicable to nouns of the singular number only; yet a collective noun, being singular in form, is sometimes preceded by this article even when it conveys the idea of plurality and takes a plural verb: as, "There *are* a very great *number* [of adverbs] ending in *ly*."—*Buchanan's Syntax*, p. 63. "A *plurality* of them *are* sometimes felt at the same instant."—*Kames, El. of Crit.*, Vol. i, p. 114. In support of this construction, it would be easy to adduce a great multitude of examples from the most reputable writers; but still, as it seems not very consistent, to take any word plurally after restricting it to the singular, we ought rather to avoid this if we can, and prefer words that literally agree in number: as, "Of adverbs there *are* very *many* ending in *ly*"—"*More than one* of them *are* sometimes felt at the same instant." The word *plurality*, like other collective nouns, is literally singular: as, "To produce the latter, a *plurality* of objects *is* necessary."—*Kames, El. of Crit.*, Vol. i, p. 224.

OBS. 13.—Respecting the form of the indefinite article, present practice differs a little from that of our ancient writers. *An* was formerly used before all words beginning with *h*, and before several other words which are now pronounced in such a manner as to require *a*: thus, we read in the Bible, "*An* help,"—"*an* house,"—"*an* hundred,"—"*an* one,"—"*an* ewer,"—"*an* usurer;" whereas we now say, "*A* help,"—"*a* house,"—"*a* hundred,"—"*a* one,"—"*a* ewer,"—"*a* usurer."

OBS. 14.—Before the word *humble*, with its compounds and derivatives, some use *an*, and others, *a*; according to their practice, in this instance, of sounding or suppressing the aspiration. Webster and Jameson sound the *h*, and consequently prefer *a*; as, "But *a humbling* image is not always necessary to produce that effect."—*Kames, El. of Crit.*, i, 205. "O what a blessing is *a humble* mind!"—*Christian Experience*, p. 342. But Sheridan, Walker, Perry, Jones, and perhaps a majority of fashionable speakers, leave the *h* silent, and would consequently say, "*An humbling* image,"—"*an humble* mind,"—&c.

OBS. 15.—An observance of the principles on which the article is to be repeated or not repeated in a sentence, is of very great moment in respect to accuracy of composition. These principles are briefly stated in the notes below, but it is proper that the learner should know the reasons of the distinctions which are there made. By a repetition of the article before several adjectives in the same construction, a repetition of the noun is implied; but without a repetition of the article, the adjectives, in all fairness of interpretation, are confined to one and the same noun: as, "No figures will render *a cold* or *an empty* composition interesting."—*Blair's Rhet.*, p. 134. Here the author speaks of a cold composition and an empty composition as different things. "*The* metaphorical and *the* literal meaning *are* improperly mixed."—*Murray's Gram.*, p. 339. Here the verb are has two nominatives, one of which is expressed, and the other understood. "But *the* third and *the* last of these [forms] are seldom used."—*Adam's Lat. Gram.*, p. 186. Here the verb "*are used*" has two nominatives, both of which are understood; namely, "the third *form*," and "the last *form*." Again: "*The original and present* signification *is* always retained."—*Dr. Murray's Hist. of Lang.*, Vol. ii, p. 149. Here *one signification* is characterized as being both original and present. "*A loose and verbose manner* never *fails* to create disgust."—*Blair's Rhet.*, p. 261. That is, *one manner,* loose and verbose. "To give *a* short and yet clear and plain answer to this proposition."—

Barclay's Works, Vol. i, p. 533. That is, *one answer, short, clear, and plain*; for the conjunctions in the text connect nothing but the adjectives.

OBS. 16.—To avoid repetition, even of the little word *the,* we sometimes, with one article, join *inconsistent* qualities to a *plural noun*;—that is, when the adjectives so differ as to individualize the things, we sometimes make the noun plural, in stead of repeating the article: as, "*The* north and south *poles*;" in stead of, "*The* north and *the* south *pole*."—"*The* indicative and potential *moods*;" in stead of "*The* indicative and *the* potential *mood*."—"*The* Old and New *Testaments*;" in stead of, "*The* Old and *the* New *Testament*." But, in any such case, to repeat the article when the noun is made plural, is a huge blunder; because it implies a repetition of the plural noun. And again, not to repeat the article when the noun is singular, is also wrong; because it forces the adjectives to coalesce in describing one and the same thing. Thus, to say, "*The* north and south *pole*" is certainly wrong, unless we mean by it, *one pole,* or *slender stick of wood,* pointing north and south; and again, to say, "*The* north and *the* south *poles,*" is also wrong, unless we mean by it, *several poles at the north* and *others at the south.* So the phrase, "*The* Old and New *Testament*" is wrong, because we have not *one Testament that is both Old and New*; and again, "*The* Old and *the* New *Testaments,*" is wrong, because we have not several *Old Testaments and several New ones*: at least we have them not in the Bible.

OBS. 17.—Sometimes a noun that *admits no article,* is preceded by adjectives that do not describe the same thing; as, "Never to jumble *metaphorical and plain language* together."—*Blair's Rhet.,* p. 146. This means, "*metaphorical language* and *plain language*;" and, for the sake of perfect clearness, it would perhaps be better to express it so. "For as *intrinsic and relative beauty* must often be blended in the same building, it becomes a difficult task to attain *both* in any perfection."—*Karnes, El. of Crit.,* Vol. ii, p. 330. That is, "*intrinsic beauty* and *relative beauty*" must often be blended; and this phraseology would be better. "In correspondence to that distinction of *male and female sex*."—*Blair's Rhet.*, p. 74. This may be expressed as well or better, in half a dozen other ways; for the article may be added, or the noun may be made plural, with or without the article, and before or after the adjectives. "They make no distinction between causes of civil and criminal jurisdiction."— *Adams's Rhet.*, Vol. i, p. 302. This means—"between causes of civil and *causes* of criminal jurisdiction;" and, for the sake of perspicuity, it ought to have been so written,—or, still better, *thus*: "They make no distinction between civil causes and criminal."

NOTES TO RULE I.

NOTE I.—When the indefinite article is required, *a* should always be used before the sound of a consonant, and *an*, before that of a vowel; as, "With the talents of *an* angel, a man may be *a* fool."—*Young*.

NOTE II.—The article *an* or *a* must never be so used as to relate, or even seem to relate, to a plural noun. The following sentence is therefore faulty: "I invited her to spend a day in viewing *a seat and gardens*."—*Rambler*, No. 34. Say, "a seat and *its* gardens."

NOTE III.—When nouns are joined in construction, with different adjuncts, different dependence, or positive contrast, the article, if it belong at all to the latter, must be repeated. The following sentence is therefore inaccurate: "She never considered the quality, but merit of her visitors."—*Wm. Penn.* Say, "*the* merit." So the article in brackets is absolutely necessary to the sense and propriety of the following phrase, though not inserted by the learned author: "The Latin introduced between the Conquest and [*the*] reign of Henry the Eighth."—*Fowler's E. Gram.*, 8vo, 1850, p. 42.

NOTE IV.—When adjectives are connected, and the qualities belong to things individually different, though of the same name, the article should be repeated: as, "*A* black and *a* white horse;"—i. e., *two horses*, one black and the other white. "*The* north and *the* south line;"—i. e., *two lines*, running east and west.

NOTE V.—When adjectives are connected, and the qualities all belong to the same thing or things, the article should not be repeated: as, "*A* black and white horse;"—i. e., *one* horse, *piebald*. "*The* north and south line;"—i. e., *one line*, running north and south, like a meridian. NOTE VI.—When two or more individual things of the same name are distinguished by adjectives that cannot unite to describe the same thing, the article must be added to each if the noun be singular, and to the first only if the noun follow them in the plural: as, "*The* nominative and *the* objective *case*;" or, "*The* nominative and objective *cases*."—"*The* third, *the* fifth, *the* seventh, and *the* eighth *chapter*;" or, "*The* third, fifth, seventh, and eighth *chapters*." [338]

NOTE VII.—When two phrases of the same sentence have any special correspondence with each other, the article, if used in the former, is in general required also in the latter: as, "For ye know neither *the* day nor *the* hour."—*Matt.*, xxv, 13. "Neither *the* cold nor *the* fervid are formed for friendship."—*Murray's Key*, p. 209. "The vail of the temple was rent in twain, from *the* top to *the* bottom."—*Matt.*, xxvii, 51.

NOTE VIII.—When a special correspondence is formed between individual epithets, the noun which follows must not be made plural; because the article, in such a case, cannot be repeated as the construction of correspondents requires. Thus, it is improper to say, "Both *the* first and second *editions*" or, "Both *the* first and *the* second *editions*" for the accurate phrase, "Both *the* first and *the* second *edition*;" and still worse to say, "Neither *the* Old nor New *Testaments*" or, "Neither *the* Old nor *the* New

Testaments" for the just expression, "Neither *the* Old nor *the* New *Testament*." Yet we may say, "Neither *the old* nor *the new statutes*" or, "Both *the early* and *the late editions*;" for here the epithets severally apply to more than one thing.

NOTE IX.—In a series of three or more terms, if the article is used with any, it should in general be added either to every one, or else to the first only. The following phrase is therefore inaccurate: "Through their attention to the helm, the sails, or rigging."—*Brown's Estimate*, Vol. i, p. 11. Say, "*the* rigging."

NOTE X.—As the article *an* or *a* denotes "*one thing of a kind*," it should not be used as we use *the,* to denote emphatically a *whole kind*; and again, when the species is said to be *of the genus,* no article should be used to limit the latter. Thus some will say, "*A jay* is a sort of *a bird*;" whereas they ought to say, "*The jay* is a sort *of bird*." Because it is absurd to suggest, that *one jay* is *a sort* of *one bird*. Yet we may say, "*The jay* is *a bird*," or, "*A jay* is *a bird*;" because, as every species is one under the genus, so every individual is one under both.

NOTE XI.—The article should not be used before the names of virtues, vices, passions, arts, or sciences, in their general sense; before terms that are strictly limited by other definitives; or before any noun whose signification is sufficiently definite without it: as, "*Falsehood* is odious."—"*Iron* is useful."—"*Beauty* is vain."—"*Admiration* is useless, when it is not supported by *domestic worth*"—*Webster's Essays,* p. 30.

NOTE XII.—When titles are mentioned merely as titles; or names of things, merely as names or words; the article should not be used before them: as, "He is styled *Marquis*;" not, "*the* Marquis," or, "*a* Marquis,"—"Ought a teacher to call his pupil *Master*?"—"*Thames* is derived from the Latin name *Tam~esis*."

NOTE XIII.—When a comparison or an alternative is made with two nouns, if both of them refer to the same subject, the article should not be inserted before the latter; if to different subjects, it should not be omitted: thus, if we say, "He is a better teacher than poet," we compare different qualifications of the same man; but if we say, "He is a better teacher than *a* poet," we speak of different men, in regard to the same qualification.

NOTE XIV.—The definite article, or some other definitive, (as *this, that, these, those*,) is generally required before the antecedent to the pronoun *who* or *which* in a restrictive clause; as, "All *the men who* were present, agreed to it."—*W. Allen's Gram.*, p. 145. "The *thoughts which* passion suggests are always plain and obvious ones."—*Blair's Rhet.*, p. 468. "The *things which* are impossible with men, are possible with God."—*Luke*, xviii, 27. See Etymology, Chap. V, Obs. 26th, &c., on Classes of Pronouns.

NOTE XV.—The article is generally required in that construction which converts a participle into a verbal or participial noun; as, "*The completing of* this, by *the working-out of* sin inherent, must be by the power and spirit of Christ in the heart."—*Wm. Penn.* "They shall be *an abhorring* unto all flesh."—*Isaiah*, lxvi, 24. "For *the dedicating of* the altar."—*Numb.*, vii, 11.

NOTE XVI.—The article should not be added to any participle that is not taken in all other respects as a noun; as, "For *the* dedicating the altar."—"He made a mistake in *the* giving out the text." Expunge *the*, and let *dedicating* and *giving* here stand as participles only; for in the construction of nouns, they must have not only a definitive before them, but the preposition *of* after them.

NOTE XVII.—The false syntax of articles properly includes every passage in which there is any faulty insertion, omission, choice, or position, of this part of speech. For example: "When the verb is *a* passive, the agent and object change places."—*Lowth's Gram.*, p. 73. Better: "When the verb is *passive*, the agent and *the* object change places." "Comparisons used by the sacred poets, are generally short."—*Russell's Gram.*, p. 87. Better: "*The* comparisons," &c. "Pronoun means *for noun*, and *is used* to *avoid the* too frequent repetition of *the* noun."—*Infant School Gram.*, p. 89. Say rather: "*The* pronoun *is put* for *a* noun, and is used to *prevent* too frequent a repetition of the noun." Or: "*The word* PRONOUN means *for noun*; and *a pronoun* is used to prevent too frequent a repetition of *some* noun."

IMPROPRIETIES FOR CORRECTION. FALSE SYNTAX UNDER RULE I.

[Fist][The examples of False Syntax placed under the rules and notes, are to be corrected *orally* by the pupil, according to the formules given, or according to others framed in like manner, and adapted to the several notes.]

EXAMPLES UNDER NOTE I.—AN OR A.

"I have seen an horrible thing in the house of Israel."—*Hosea*, vi, 10.

[FORMULE.—Not proper, because the article *an* is used before *horrible*, which begins with the sound of the consonant *h*. But, according to Note 1st, under Rule 1st, "When the indefinite article is required, *a* should always be used before the sound of a consonant, and *an*, before that of a vowel." Therefore, *an* should be *a*; thus, "I have seen *a* horrible thing in the house of Israel."]

"There is an harshness in the following sentences."—*Priestley's Gram.*, p. 188. "Indeed, such an one is not to be looked for."—*Blair's Rhet.*, p. 27. "If each of you will be disposed to approve himself an useful citizen."—*Ib.*, p. 263. "Land with them had acquired almost an European value."—

Webster's Essays, p. 325. "He endeavoured to find out an wholesome remedy."—*Neef's Method of Ed.*, p. 3. "At no time have we attended an Yearly Meeting more to our own satisfaction."—*The Friend*, v, 224. "Addison was not an humourist in character."—*Kames, El. of Crit.*, i, 303. "Ah me! what an one was he?"—*Lily's Gram.*, p. 49. "He was such an one as I never saw."—*Ib.* "No man can be a good preacher, who is not an useful one."—*Blair's Rhet.*, p. 283. "An usage which is too frequent with Mr. Addison."—*Ib.*, p. 200. "Nobody joins the voice of a sheep with the shape of an horse."—*Locke's Essay*, p. 298. "An universality seems to be aimed at by the omission of the article."—*Priestley's Gram.*, p. 154. "Architecture is an useful as well as a fine art."—*Kames, El. of Crit.*, ii, 335. "Because the same individual conjunctions do not preserve an uniform signification."—*Nutting's Gram.*, p. 78. "Such a work required the patience and assiduity of an hermit."—*Johnson's Life of Morin.* "Resentment is an union of sorrow with malignity."—*Rambler*, No. 185. "His bravery, we know, was an high courage of blasphemy."—*Pope.* "Hyssop; a herb of bitter taste."—*Pike's Heb. Lex.*, p. 3.

"On each enervate string they taught the note
To pant, or tremble through an Eunuch's throat."—*Pope.*

UNDER NOTE II.—AN OR A WITH PLURALS.

"At a sessions of the court in March, it was moved," &c.—*Hutchinson's Hist. of Mass.*, i, 61. "I shall relate my conversations, of which I kept a memoranda."—*Duchess D'Abrantes*, p. 26. "I took another dictionary, and with a scissors cut out, for instance, the word ABACUS."—*A. B. Johnson's Plan of a Dict.*, p. 12. "A person very meet seemed he for the purpose, of a forty-five years old."—*Gardiner's Music of Nature*, p. 338. "And it came to pass about an eight days after these sayings."—*Luke*, ix, 28." There were slain of them upon a three thousand men."—*1 Mac.*, iv, 15." Until I had gained the top of these white mountains, which seemed another Alps of snow."—*Addison, Tat.*, No. 161. "To make them a satisfactory amends for all the losses they had sustained."—*Goldsmith's Greece*, p. 187. "As a first fruits of many more that shall be gathered."—*Barclay's Works*, i, 506. "It makes indeed a little amends, by inciting us to oblige people."—*Sheffield's Works*, ii, 229. "A large and lightsome backstairs leads up to an entry above."—*Ib.*, p. 260. "Peace of mind is an honourable amends for the sacrifices of interest."—*Murray's Gram.*, p. 162; *Smith's*, 138. "With such a spirit and sentiments were hostilities carried on."—*Robertson's America*, i, 166. "In the midst of a thick woods, he had long lived a voluntary recluse."—*G. B.* "The flats look almost like a young woods."—*Morning Chronicle.* "As we went on, the country for a little ways improved, but scantily."—*Essex County Freeman*, Vol. ii, No. 11. "Whereby the Jews were permitted to return into their own country, after a seventy years captivity at Babylon."—*Rollin's An. Hist.*, Vol. ii, p. 20. "He did riot go a great ways into the country."—*Gilbert's Gram.*, p. 85.

"A large amends by fortune's hand is made,
    And the lost Punic blood is well repay'd."—*Rowe's Lucan*, iv, 1241.

UNDER NOTE III.—NOUNS CONNECTED.

"As where a landscape is conjoined with the music of birds and odour of flowers."—*Kames, El. of Crit.*, i, 117. "The last order resembles the second in the mildness of its accent, and softness of its pause."—*Ib.*, ii, 113. "Before the use of the loadstone or knowledge of the compass."—*Dryden.* "The perfect participle and imperfect tense ought not to be confounded."—*Murray's Gram.*, ii, 292. "In proportion as the taste of a poet, or orator, becomes more refined."—*Blair's Rhet.*, p. 27. "A situation can never be intricate, as long as there is an angel, devil, or musician, to lend a helping hand."—*Kames, El. of Crit.*, ii, 285. "Avoid rude sports: an eye is soon lost, or bone broken."—"Not a word was uttered, nor sign given."—*Brown's Inst.*, p. 125. "I despise not the doer, but deed."—*Ibid.* "For the sake of an easier pronunciation and more agreeable sound."—*Lowth.* "The levity as well as loquacity of the Greeks made them incapable of keeping up the true standard of history."—*Bolingbroke, on Hist.*, p. 115.

UNDER NOTE IV.—ADJECTIVES CONNECTED.

"It is proper that the vowels be a long and short one."—*Murray's Gram.*, p. 327. "Whether the person mentioned was seen by the speaker a long or short time before."—*Ib.*, p. 70; *Fisk's*, 72. "There are three genders, Masculine, Feminine, and Neuter."—*Adam's Lat. Gram.*, p. 8. "The numbers are two; Singular and Plural."—*Ib.*, p. 80; *Gould's*, 77. "The persons are three; First, Second, [and] Third."—*Adam, et al.* "Nouns and pronouns have three cases; the nominative, possessive, and objective."—*Comly's Gram.*, p. 19; *Ingersoll's*, 21. "Verbs have five moods; namely, the Indicative, Potential, Subjunctive, Imperative, and Infinitive."—*Bullions's E. Gram.*, p. 35; *Lennie's*, 20. "How many numbers have pronouns? Two, the singular and plural."—*Bradley's Gram.*, p. 82. "To distinguish between an interrogative and exclamatory sentence."—*Murray's Gram.*, p. 280; *Comly's*, 163; *Ingersoll's*, 292. "The first and last of which are compounded members."—*Lowth's Gram.*, p. 123. "In the last lecture, I treated of the concise and diffuse, the nervous and feeble manner."—*Blair's Rhet.*, p. 183. "The passive and neuter verbs, I shall reserve for some future conversation."—*Ingersoll's Gram.*, p. 69. "There are two voices; the Active and Passive."—*Adam's Gram.*, p. 59; *Gould's*, 87. "Whose is rather the poetical than regular genitive of *which*."—*Dr. Johnson's Gram.*, p. 7. "To feel the force of a compound, or derivative word."—*Town's Analysis*, p. 4.

"To preserve the distinctive uses of the copulative and disjunctive conjunctions."—*Murray's Gram.*, p. 150; *Ingersoll's*, 233. "E has a long and short sound in most languages."— *Bicknell's Gram.*, Part ii, p. 13. "When the figurative and literal sense are mixed and jumbled together."—*Blair's Rhet.*, p. 151. "The Hebrew, with which the Canaanitish and Phoenician stand in connection."—CONANT: *Fowler's E. Gram.*, 8vo, 1850, p. 28. "The languages of Scandinavia proper, the Norwegian and Swedish."— *Fowler, ib.*, p. 31.

UNDER NOTE V.—ADJECTIVES CONNECTED.

"The path of truth is a plain and a safe path"—*Murray's Key*, p. 236. "Directions for acquiring a just and a happy elocution."—*Kirkham's Elocution*, p. 144. "Its leading object is to adopt a correct and an easy method."—*Kirkham's Gram.*, p. 9. "How can it choose but wither in a long and a sharp winter."—*Cowley's Pref.*, p. vi. "Into a dark and a distant unknown."—*Chalmers, on Astronomy*, p. 230. "When the bold and the strong enslaved his fellow man."—*Chazotte's Essay*, p. 21. "We now proceed to consider the things most essential to an accurate and a perfect sentence." —*Murray's Gram.*, p. 306. "And hence arises a second and a very considerable source of the improvement of taste."—*Blair's Rhet.*, p. 18. "Novelty produces in the mind a vivid and an agreeable emotion."—*Ib.*, p. 50. "The deepest and the bitterest feeling still is, the separation."— *Dr. M'Rie.* "A great and a good man looks beyond time."—*Brown's Institutes*, p. 125. "They made but a weak and an ineffectual resistance." —*Ib.* "The light and the worthless kernels will float."—*Ib.* "I rejoice that there is an other and a better world."—*Ib.* "For he is determined to *revise* his work, and present to the publick another and a better edition."—*Kirkham's Gram.*, p. 7. "He hoped that this title would secure him an ample and an independent authority."—*Murray's Gram.*, p. 172: see *Priestley's*, 147. "There is however another and a more limited sense."—*Adams's Rhet.*, Vol. ii, p. 232.

UNDER NOTE VI.—ARTICLES OR PLURALS.

"This distinction forms, what are called the diffuse and the concise styles."—*Blair's Rhet.*, p. 176. "Two different modes of speaking, distinguished at first by the denominations of the Attic and the Asiatic manners."—*Adams's Rhet.*, Vol. i, p. 83. "But the great design of uniting the Spanish and the French monarchies under the former was laid."—*Bolingbroke, on History*, p. 180. "In the solemn and the poetic styles, it [*do* or *did*] is often rejected."—*W. Allen's Gram.*, p. 68. "They cannot be at the same time in the objective and the nominative cases."—*Murray's Gram.*, 8vo, p. 151; *Ingersoll's*, 239; *R. G. Smith's*, 127. "They are named the POSITIVE, the COMPARATIVE, and the SUPERLATIVE degrees."—*Smart's Accidence*, p. 27. "Certain Adverbs are capable of taking an Inflection, namely, that of the comparative and the superlative degrees."—*Fowler's E. Gram.*, 8vo, 1850, §321. "In the subjunctive mood, the present and the imperfect tenses often carry with them a future sense."—*L. Murray's Gram.*, p. 187; *Fisk's*, 131. "The imperfect, the perfect, the pluperfect, and the first future tenses of this mood, are conjugated like the same tenses of the indicative."—*Kirkham's Gram.*, p. 145. "What rules apply in parsing personal pronouns of the second and third person?"—*Ib.*, p. 116. "Nouns are sometimes in the nominative or objective case after the neuter verb to be, or after an active-intransitive or passive verb."—*Ib.*, p. 55. "The verb varies its endings in the singular in order to agree in form with the first, second, and third person of its nominative."—*Ib.*, p. 47. "They are identical in effect, with the radical and the vanishing stresses."—*Rush, on the Voice*, p. 339. "In a sonnet the first, fourth, fifth, and eighth line rhyme to each other: so do the second, third, sixth, and seventh line; the ninth, eleventh, and thirteenth line; and the tenth, twelfth, and fourteenth line."—*Churchill's Gram.*, p. 311. "The iron and the golden ages are run; youth and manhood are departed."—*Wright's Athens,* p. 74. "If, as you say, the iron and the golden ages are past, the youth and the manhood of the world."—*Ib.* "An Exposition of the Old and New Testament."—*Matthew Henry's Title-page.* "The names and order of the books of the Old and New Testament."—*Friends' Bible,* p. 2; *Bruce's,* p. 2; et al. "In the second and third person of that tense."—*L. Murray's Gram.*, p. 81. "And who still unites in himself the human and the divine natures."—*Gurney's Evidences,* p. 59. "Among whom arose the Italian, the Spanish, the French, and the English languages."—*L. Murray's Gram.*, 8vo, p. 111. "Whence arise these two, the singular and the plural Numbers."—*Burn's Gram.*, p. 32.

UNDER NOTE VII.—CORRESPONDENT TERMS.

"Neither the definitions, nor examples, are entirely the same with his."—*Ward's Pref. to Lily's Gram.*, p. vi. "Because it makes a discordance between the thought and expression."—*Kames, El. of Crit.*, ii, 24. "Between the adjective and following substantive."—*Ib.* ii, 104. "Thus, Athens became both the repository and nursery of learning."—*Chazotte's Essay,* p. 28. "But the French pilfered from both the Greek and Latin."—*Ib.*, p. 102. "He shows that Christ is both the power and wisdom of God."—*The Friend,* x, 414. "That he might be Lord both of the dead and living."—*Rom.*, xiv, 9. "This is neither the obvious nor grammatical meaning of his words."—*Blair's Rhet.*, p. 209. "Sometimes both the accusative and infinitive are understood."—*Adam's Gram.*, p. 155; *Gould's,* 158. "In some cases we can use either the nominative or accusative promiscuously."—*Adam,* p. 156; *Gould,* 159. "Both the former and latter substantive are sometimes to be understood."—*Adam,* p. 157; *Gould,* 160. "Many whereof have escaped both the commentator and poet himself."—*Pope.* "The verbs must and ought have both a present and past signification."—*Murray's Gram.*, p. 108. "How shall we distinguish between the friends and enemies of the government?"—*Webster's Essays*, p. 352. "Both the ecclesiastical and secular powers concurred in those measures."—*Campbell's Rhet.*, p. 260. "As the period has a beginning and end within itself it implies an inflexion."—*Adams's Rhet.*, ii, 245. "Such as ought to subsist between a principal and accessory."—*Kames, on Crit.*, ii, 39.

UNDER NOTE VIII.—CORRESPONDENCE PECULIAR.

"When both the upward and the downward slides occur in pronouncing a syllable, they are called a *Circumflex* or *Wave*."—*Kirkham's Elocution*, pp. 75 and 104. "The word *that* is used both in the nominative and objective cases."—*Sanborn's Gram.*, p. 69. "But all the other moods and tenses of the verbs, both in the active and passive voices, are conjugated at large."—*Murray's Gram.*, 8vo, p. 81. "Some writers on Grammar object to the propriety of admitting the second future, in both the indicative and subjunctive moods."—*Ib.*, p. 82. "The same conjunction governing both the indicative and the subjunctive moods, in the same sentence, and in the same circumstances, seems to be a great impropriety."—*Ib.*, p. 207. "The true distinction between the subjunctive and the indicative moods in this tense."—*Ib.*, p. 208. "I doubt of his capacity to teach either the French or English languages."—*Chazotte's Essay*, p. 7. "It is as necessary to make a distinction between the active transitive and the active intransitive forms of the verb, as between the active and passive forms."—*Nixon's Parser*, p. 13.

UNDER NOTE IX.—A SERIES OF TERMS.

"As comprehending the terms uttered by the artist, the mechanic, and husbandman."—*Chazotte's Essay*, p. 24. "They may be divided into four classes—the Humanists, Philanthropists, Pestalozzian and the Productive Schools."—*Smith's New Gram.*, p. iii. "Verbs have six tenses, the Present, the Imperfect, the Perfect, the Pluperfect, and the First and Second Future tenses."—*Kirkham's Gram.*, p. 138; *L. Murray's*, 68; *R. C. Smith's*, 27; *Alger's*, 28. "*Is* is an irregular verb neuter, indicative mood, present tense, and the third person singular."—*Murray's Gram.*, Vol. ii, p. 2. "*Should give* is an irregular verb active, in the potential mood, the imperfect tense, and the first person plural."—*Ibid.* "*Us* is a personal pronoun, first person plural, and in the objective case."—*Ibid.* "*Them* is a personal pronoun, of the third person, the plural number, and in the objective case."—*Ibid.* "It is surprising that the Jewish critics, with all their skill in dots, points, and accents, never had the ingenuity to invent a point of interrogation, of admiration, or a parenthesis."—*Wilson's Hebrew Gram.*, p. 47. "The fifth, sixth, seventh, and the eighth verse."—*O. B. Peirce's Gram.*, p. 263. "Substitutes have three persons; the First, Second, and the Third."—*Ib.*, p. 34. "*John's* is a proper noun, of the masculine gender, the third person, singular number, possessive case, and governed by *wife*, by Rule I."—*Smith's New Gram.*, p. 48. "Nouns in the English language have three cases; the nominative, the possessive, and objective."—*Barrett's Gram.*, p. 13; *Alexander's*, 11. "The Potential [mood] has four [tenses], viz. the Present, the Imperfect, the Perfect, and Pluperfect."—*Ingersoll's Gram.*, p. 96.

"Where Science, Law, and Liberty depend,
And own the patron, patriot, and the friend."—*Savage, to Walpole*.

UNDER NOTE X.—SPECIES AND GENUS.

"A pronoun is a part of speech put for a noun."—*Paul's Accidence*, p. 11. "A verb is a part of speech declined with mood and tense."—*Ib.*, p. 15. "A participle is a part of speech derived of a verb."—*Ib.*, p. 38. "An adverb is a part of speech joined to verbs to declare their signification."—*Ib.*, p. 40. "A conjunction is a part of speech that joineth sentences together."—*Ib.*, p. 41. "A preposition is a part of speech most commonly set before other parts."—*Ib.*, p. 42. "An interjection is a part of speech which betokeneth a sudden motion or passion of the mind."—*Ib.*, p. 44. "An enigma or riddle is also a species of allegory."—*Blair's Rhet.*, p. 151; *Murray's Gram.*, 343. "We may take from the Scriptures a very fine example of an allegory."—*Ib.*: *Blair*, 151; *Mur.*, 341. "And thus have you exhibited a sort of a sketch of art."—HARRIS: *in Priestley's Gram.*, p. 176. "We may 'imagine a subtle kind of a reasoning,' as Mr. Harris acutely observes."—*Churchill's Gram.*, p. 71. "But, before entering on these, I shall give one instance of a very beautiful metaphor, that I may show the figure to full advantage."—*Blair's Rhet.*, p. 143. "Aristotle, in his Poetics, uses metaphor in this extended sense, for any figurative meaning imposed upon a word; as a whole put for the part, or a part for a whole; the species for the genus, or a genus for the species."—*Ib.*, p. 142. "It shows what kind of an apple it is of which we are speaking."—*Kirkham's Gram.*, p. 69. "Cleon was another sort of a man."—*Goldsmith's Greece*, Vol. i, p. 124. "To keep off his right wing, as a kind of a reserved body."—*Ib.*, ii, 12. "This part of speech is called a verb."—*Mack's Gram.*, p. 70. "What sort of a thing is it?"—*Hiley's Gram.*, p. 20. "What sort of a charm do they possess?"—*Bullions's Principles of E. Gram.*, p. 73.

"Dear Welsted, mark, in dirty hole,
  That painful animal, a Mole."—*Note to Dunciad*, B. ii, l. 207.

UNDER NOTE XI.—ARTICLES NOT REQUISITE.

"Either thou or the boys were in the fault."—*Comly's Key, in Gram.*, p. 174. "It may, at the first view, appear to be too general."—*Murray's Gram.*, p. 222; *Ingersoll's*, 275. "When the verb has a reference to future time."—*Ib.*:

M., p. 207; *Ing.*, 264. "No; they are the language of imagination rather than of a passion."—*Blair's Rhet.*, p. 165. "The dislike of the English Grammar, which has so generally prevailed, can only be attributed to the intricacy of syntax."—*Russell's Gram.*, p. iv. "Is that ornament in a good taste?"—*Kames, El. of Crit.*, ii, 326. "There are not many fountains in a good taste."—*Ib.*, ii, 329. "And I persecuted this way unto the death."—*Acts*, xxii, 4. "The sense of the feeling can, indeed, give us the idea of extension."—*Blair's Rhet.*, p. 196. "The distributive adjective pronouns, *each, every, either*, agree with the nouns, pronouns, and verbs, of the singular number only."—*Murray's Gram.*, p. 165; *Lowth's*, 89. "Expressing by one word, what might, by a circumlocution, be resolved into two or more words belonging to the other parts of speech."—*Blair's Rhet.*, p. 84. "By the certain muscles which operate all at the same time."—*Murray's Gram.*, p. 19. "It is sufficient here to have observed thus much in the general concerning them."—*Campbell's Rhet.*, p. 112. "Nothing disgusts us sooner than the empty pomp of language."—*Murray's Gram.*, p. 319.

UNDER NOTE XII.—TITLES AND NAMES.

"He is entitled to the appellation of a gentleman."—*Brown's Inst.*, p. 126. "Cromwell assumed the title of a Protector."—*Ib.* "Her father is honoured with the title of an Earl."—*Ib.* "The chief magistrate is styled a President."—*Ib.* "The highest title in the state is that of the Governor."—*Ib.* "That boy is known by the name of the Idler."—*Murray's Key*, 8vo, p. 205. "The one styled the Mufti, is the head of the ministers of law and religion."—*Balbi's Geog.*, p. 360. "Banging all that possessed them under one class, he called that whole class *a tree*."—*Blair's Rhet.*, p. 73. "For the oak, the pine, and the ash, were names of whole classes of objects."—*Ib.*, p. 73. "It is of little importance whether we give to some particular mode of expression the name of a trope, or of a figure."—*Ib.*, p. 133. "The collision of a vowel with itself is the most ungracious of all combinations, and has been doomed to peculiar reprobation under the name of an hiatus."—*J. Q. Adams's Rhet.*, Vol. ii, p. 217. "We hesitate to determine, whether the *Tyrant* alone, is the nominative, or whether the nominative includes the spy."—*Cobbett's E. Gram.*, ¶ 246. "Hence originated the customary abbreviation of *twelve months* into a *twelve-month*; *seven nights* into *se'night*; *fourteen nights* into a *fortnight*."—*Webster's Improved Gram.*, p. 105.

UNDER NOTE XIII.—COMPARISONS AND ALTERNATIVES.

"He is a better writer than a reader."—*W. Allen's False Syntax, Gram.*, p. 332. "He was an abler mathematician than a linguist."—*Ib.* "I should rather have an orange than apple."—*Brown's Inst.*, p. 126. "He was no less able a negotiator, than a courageous warrior."—*Smollett's Voltaire*, Vol. i, p. 181. "In an epic poem we pardon many negligences that would not be permitted in a sonnet or epigram."—*Kames, El. of Crit.*, Vol. i, p. 186. "That figure is a sphere, or a globe, or a ball."—*Harris's Hermes*, p. 258.

UNDER NOTE XIV.—ANTECEDENTS TO WHO OR WHICH.

"Carriages which were formerly in use, were very clumsy."—*Inst.*, p. 126. "The place is not mentioned by geographers who wrote at that time."—*Ib.* "Questions which a person asks himself in contemplation, ought to be terminated by points of interrogation."—*Murray's Gram.*, p. 279; *Comly's*, 162; *Ingersoll's*, 291. "The work is designed for the use of persons, who may think it merits a place in their Libraries."—*Murray's Gram.*, 8vo., p. iii. "That persons who think confusedly, should express themselves obscurely, is not to be wondered at."—*Ib.*, p. 298. "Grammarians who limit the number to two, or at most to three, do not reflect."—*Ib.*, p. 75. "Substantives which end in *ian*, are those that signify profession."—*Ib.*, p.

132. "To these may be added verbs, which chiefly among the poets govern the dative."—*Adam's Gram.*, p. 170; *Gould's*, 171. "Consonants are letters, which cannot be sounded without the aid of a vowel."—*Bucke's Gram.*, p. 9. "To employ the curiosity of persons who are skilled in grammar."—*Murray's Gram., Pref.*, p. iii. "This rule refers only to nouns and pronouns, which have the same bearing or relation."—*Ib.*, i, p. 204. "So that things which are seen, were not made of things which do appear."—*Heb.*, xi, 3. "Man is an imitative creature; he may utter sounds, which he has heard."—*Wilson's Essay on Gram.*, p. 21. "But men, whose business is wholly domestic, have little or no use for any language but their own."—*Webster's Essays*, p. 5.

UNDER NOTE XV.—PARTICIPIAL NOUNS.

"Great benefit may be reaped from reading of histories."—*Sewel's Hist.*, p. iii. "And some attempts were made towards writing of history."—*Bolingbroke, on Hist.*, p. 110. "It is Invading of the Priest's Office for any other to Offer it."—*Right of Tythes*, p. 200. "And thus far of forming of verbs."—*Walker's Art of Teaching*, p. 35. "And without shedding of blood is no remission."—*Heb.*, ix, 22. "For making of measures we have the best method here in England."—*Printer's Gram.* "This is really both admitting and denying, at once."—*Butler's Analogy*, p. 72. "And hence the origin of making of parliaments."—*Brown's Estimate*, Vol. i, p. 71. "Next thou objectest, that having of saving light and grace presupposes conversion. But that I deny: for, on the contrary, conversion presupposeth having light and grace."—*Barclay's Works*, Vol. i, p. 143. "They cried down wearing of rings and other superfluities as we do."—*Ib.*, i, 236. "Whose adorning, let it not be that outward adorning of plaiting the hair, and of wearing of gold, or of putting on of apparel."—*1 Peter*, iii, 3. "In spelling of derivative Words, the Primitive must be kept whole."—*British Gram.*, p. 50; *Buchanan's Syntax,*

9. "And the princes offered for dedicating of the altar."—*Numbers*, vii, 10. "Boasting is not only telling of lies, but also many unseemly truths."—*Sheffield's Works*, ii, 244. "We freely confess that forbearing of prayer in the wicked is sinful."—*Barclay*, i, 316. "For revealing of a secret, there is no remedy."—*Inst. E. Gram.*, p. 126. "He turned all his thoughts to composing of laws for the good of the state."—*Rollin's Ancient Hist.*, Vol. ii, p. 38.

UNDER NOTE XVI.—PARTICIPLES, NOT NOUNS. "It is salvation to be kept from falling into a pit, as truly as to be taken out of it after the falling in."—*Barclay*, i, 210. "For in the receiving and embracing the testimony of truth, they felt eased."—*Ib.*, i, 469. "True regularity does not consist in the having but a single rule, and forcing every thing to conform to it."—*Philol. Museum*, i, 664. "To the man of the world, this sound of glad tidings appears only an idle tale, and not worth the attending to."—*Life of Tho. Say*, p. 144. "To be the deliverer of the captive Jews, by the ordering their temple to be re-built," &c.—*Rollin*, ii, 124. "And for the preserving them from being defiled."—*N. E. Discipline*, p. 133. "A wise man will avoid the showing any excellence in trifles."—*Art of Thinking*, p. 80. "Hirsutus had no other reason for the valuing a book."—*Rambler*, No. 177; *Wright's Gram.*, p. 190. "To the being heard with satisfaction, it is necessary that the speaker should deliver himself with ease."—*Sheridan's Elocution*, p. 114. "And to the being well heard, and clearly understood, a good and distinct articulation contributes more, than power of voice."—*Ib.*, p. 117.

"*Potential* means the having power or will;
As, If you *would* improve, you *should* be still."
—*Tobitt's Gram.*, p. 31.

UNDER NOTE XVII.—VARIOUS ERRORS.

"For the same reason, a neuter verb cannot become a passive."—*Lowth's Gram.*, p. 74. "The period is the whole sentence complete in itself."—*Ib.*, p. 115. "The colon or member is a chief constructive part, or greater division of a sentence."—*Ib.* "The semicolon or half member, is a less constructive part or subdivision, of a sentence or member."—*Ib.* "A sentence or member is again subdivided into commas or segments."—*Ib.*, p. 116. "The first error that I would mention, is, a too general attention to the dead languages, with a neglect of our own."—*Webster's Essays*, p. 3. "One third of the importations would supply the demands of people."—*Ib.*, p. 119. "And especially in grave stile."—*Priestley's Gram.*, p. 72. "By too eager pursuit, he ran a great risk of being disappointed."—*Murray's Key, Octavo Gram.*, Vol. ii, p. 201. "Letters are divided into vowels and consonants."—*Murray's Gram.*, i, p. 7; *and others*. "Consonants are divided into mutes and semi-vowels."—*Ib.*, i, 8; *and others*. "The first of these forms is most agreeable to the English idiom."—*Ib.*, i, 176. "If they gain, it is a too dear rate."—*Barclay's Works*, i, 504. "A pronoun is a word used instead of a noun, to prevent a too frequent repetition of it."—*Maunder's Gram.*, p. 1. "This vulgar error might perhaps arise from a too partial fondness for the Latin."—*Dr. Ash's Gram., Pref.*, p. iv. "The groans which a too heavy load extorts from her."—*Hitchcock, on Dyspepsy*, p. 50. "The numbers [of a verb] are, of course, singular and plural."—*Bucke's Gram.* p. 58. "To brook no meanness, and to stoop to no dissimulation, are the indications of a great mind."—*Murray's Key*, ii, 236. "This mode of expression rather suits familiar than grave style."—*Murray's Gram.*, i, 198. "This use of the word rather suits familiar and low style."—*Priestley's Gram.*, p. 134. "According to the nature of the composition the one or other may be predominant."—*Blair's Rhet.*, p. 102. "Yet the commonness of such sentences prevents in a great measure a too early expectation of the end."—*Campbell's Rhet.*, p. 411. "An eulogy or a philippie may be pronounced by an individual of one nation upon the subject of another."—*Adams's Rhet.*, i, 298. "A French sermon, is for most part, a warm animated exhortation."—*Blair's Rhet.*, p. 288. "I do not envy those who think slavery no very pitiable a lot."—*Channing, on Emancipation*, p. 52. "The auxiliary and principal united, constitute a tense."—*Murray's Gram.*, i, 75. "There are some verbs which are defective with respect to persons."—*Ib.*, i, 109. "In youth, the habits of industry are most easily acquired."—*Murray's Key*, ii, 235. "Apostrophe (') is used in place of a letter left out."—*Bullions's Eng. Gram.*, p. 156.

CHAPTER III.—CASES, OR NOUNS.

The rules for the construction of Nouns, or Cases, are seven; hence this chapter, according to the order adopted above, reviews the series of rules from the second rule to the eighth, inclusively. Though *Nouns* are here the topic, all these seven rules apply alike to *Nouns and to Pronouns*; that is, to all the words of our language which are susceptible of *Cases*.

RULE II.—NOMINATIVES.

A Noun or a Pronoun which is the subject of a finite verb, must be in the nominative case: as, "The *Pharisees* also, *who* were covetous, heard all these things; and *they* derided him."—*Luke*, xvi, 14. "But where the *meekness* of self-knowledge veileth the front of self-respect, there look *thou* for the man whom *none* can know but *they* will honour."—*Book of Thoughts*, p. 66.

"Dost *thou* mourn Philander's fate?
I know *thou* sayst it: says thy *life* the same?"
—*Young*, N. ii, l. 22.

OBSERVATIONS ON RULE II.

OBS. 1.—To this rule, there are *no exceptions*; and nearly all nominatives, or far the greater part, are to be parsed by it. There are however *four* different ways of disposing of the nominative case. *First*, it is generally *the subject of a verb*, according to Rule 2d. *Secondly*, it may be put *in apposition* with an other nominative, according to Rule 3d. *Thirdly*, it may be put after a verb or a participle *not transitive*, according to Rule 6th. *Fourthly*, it may be put *absolute*, or may help to form a *phrase that* is *independent* of the rest of the sentence, according to Rule 8th.

OBS. 2.—The subject, or nominative, is generally placed *before* the verb; as, "*Peace dawned* upon his mind."—*Johnson.* "*What is written* in the law?"—*Bible*. But, in the following nine cases, the subject of the verb is usually placed *after* it, or after the first auxiliary: 1. When a question is asked without an interrogative pronoun in the nominative case; as, "*Shall mortals be* implacable?"—*Hooke.* "What *art thou doing*?"—*Id.* "How many loaves *have ye*?"—*Bible.* "*Are they* Israelites? so *am I*."—*Ib.*

2. When the verb is in the imperative mood; as, "*Go thou*"—"*Come ye*" But, with this mood, the pronoun is very often omitted and understood; as, "Philip saith unto him, *Come* and *see*"—*John*, i, 46. "And he saith unto them, *Be* not *affrighted*."—*Mark*, xvi, 5.

3. When an earnest wish, or other strong feeling, is expressed; as, "*May she be* happy!"—"How *were we struck*!"—*Young.* "Not as the world giveth, *give I* unto you."—*Bible.*

4. When a supposition is made without the conjunction *if;* as, "*Had they known* it;" for, "*If* they had known it."—"*Were it* true;" for, "*If* it were true."—"*Could we draw* by the covering of the grave;" for, "*If* we could draw," &c.

5. When *neither* or *nor*, signifying *and not*, precedes the verb; as, "This was his fear; *nor was his apprehension* groundless."—"Ye shall not eat of it, *neither shall ye touch* it."—*Gen.*, iii, 3.

6. When, for the sake of emphasis, some word or words are placed before the verb, which more naturally come after it; as, "Here *am I.*"—"Narrow *is* the *way.*"—"Silver and gold *have I* none; but such as I have, *give I* thee."—*Bible.*

7. When the verb has no regimen, and is itself emphatical; as, "*Echo* the *mountains* round."—*Thomson.* "After the Light Infantry *marched* the *Grenadiers*, then *followed* the *Horse.*"—*Buchanan's Syntax*, p. 71.

8. When the verbs, *say, answer, reply*, and the like, introduce the parts of a dialogue; as, "'Son of affliction,' *said Omar*, 'who art thou?' 'My name,' *replied* the *stranger*, 'is Hassan.'"—*Dr. Johnson.*

9. When the adverb *there* precedes the verb; as, "There *lived a man.*"—*Montgomery.* "In all worldly joys, there *is* a secret *wound.*"—*Owen.* This use of *there*, the general introductory adverb of place, is idiomatic, and somewhat different from the use of the same word in reference to a particular locality; as, "Because *there* was not much water *there.*"—*John*, iii, 23.

OBS. 3.—In exclamations, and some other forms of expression, a few verbs are liable to be suppressed, the ellipsis being obvious; as, "How different [is] this from the philosophy of Greece and Rome!"—DR. BEATTIE: *Murray's Sequel*, p. 127. "What a lively picture [is here] of the most disinterested and active benevolence!"—HERVEY: *ib.*, p. 94. "When Adam [spake] thus to Eve."—MILTON: *Paradise Lost*, B. iv, l. 610.

OBS. 4.—Though we often use nouns in the nominative case to show whom we address, yet the imperative verb takes no other nominative of the second person, than the simple personal pronoun, *thou, ye*, or *you*, expressed or understood. It would seem that some, who ought to know better, are liable to mistake for the subject of such a verb, the noun which we put absolute in the nominative by direct address. Of this gross error, the following is an example: "*Study boys*. In this sentence," (says its author,) "*study* is a verb of the second person, plural number, and agrees with its nominative case, *boys*—according to the rule: A verb must agree with its nominative case in number and person. *Boys* is a noun *of* the second person, plural number, masculine gender, in the nominative case to the verb study."—*Ingersoll's Gram.*, p. 17.[339] Now the fact is, that this laconic address, of three syllables, is written wrong; being made bad English for want of a comma between the two words. Without this mark, *boys* must be an objective, governed by *study*; and with it, a nominative, put absolute by direct address. But, in either case, *study* agrees with *ye* or *you* understood, and has not the noun for its subject, or nominative.

OBS. 5.—Some authors say, and if the first person be no exception, say truly: "The nominative case to a verb, unless it be a pronoun, is always of the *third* person."—*Churchill's Gram.*, p. 141. But W. B. Fowle will have all pronouns to be *adjectives*. Consequently all his verbs, of every sort, agree with nouns "expressed or understood." This, and every other absurd theory of language, can easily be made out, by means of a few perversions, which may be called corrections, and a sufficient number of interpolations, made under pretence of filling up ellipses. Thus, according to this author, "They fear," means, "They *things spoken of* fear."—*True Eng. Gram.*, p, 33. And, "*John, open* the door," or, "*Boys, stop* your noise," admits no comma. And, "Be grateful, ye children," and, "Be ye grateful children," are, in his view, every way equivalent: the comma in the former being, in his opinion, needless. See *ib.*, p. 39.

OBS. 6.—Though the nominative and objective cases of nouns do not differ in form, it is nevertheless, in the opinion of many of our grammarians, improper to place any noun in both relations at once, because this produces a confusion in the syntax of the word. Examples: "He then goes on to declare that there *are*, and distinguish *of*, four *manners* of saying *Per se*."—*Walker's Treatise of Particles*, p. xii. Better: "He then proceeds to show, that *per se* is susceptible of four different senses." "In just allegory *and* similitude there is always a propriety, or, if you choose to call it, *congruity*, in the literal sense, as well as a distinct meaning or sentiment suggested, which is called the figurative sense."—*Campbell's Philosophy of Rhetoric*, p. 291. Better: "In just allegory *or* similitude, there is always a propriety—or, if you choose to call it *so, a congruity*—in the literal sense," &c. "It must then be meant of his sins who *makes*, not of his who *becomes*, the convert."—*Atterbury's Sermons*, i, 2. Better: "It must then be meant of his sins who *makes the convert*, not of his who *becomes converted*." "Eye *hath* not *seen*, nor ear *heard*, neither *have entered* into the heart of man, *the things* which God hath prepared for them that love him."—*1 Cor.*, ii, 9. A more regular construction would be: "Eye hath not seen, nor ear heard, neither *hath it* entered into the heart of man to *conceive*, the things which God hath prepared for them that love him." The following example, from Pope, may perhaps be conceded to the poet, as an allowable ellipsis of the words "*a friend*," after *is*:

"In who obtain defence, or who defend;
In him who *is*, or him who *finds, a friend*."
—*Essay on Man*, Ep. iv, l. 60.

Dr. Lowth cites the last three examples, without suggesting any forms of correction; and says of them, "There seems to be an impropriety in these sentences, in which the same noun stands in a double capacity, performing at the same time the offices *both of the* nominative and objective case."—

Lowth's Gram., p. 73. He should have said—"*of both the* nominative and *the* objective case." Dr. Webster, citing the line, "In him who is, and him who finds, a friend," adds, "Lowth condemns this use of the noun in the nominative and objective at the same time; but *without reason,* as the cases are not distinguished in English."—*Improved Gram.*, p. 175.

OBS. 7.—In Latin and Greek, the accusative before the infinitive, is often reckoned *the subject* of the latter verb; and is accordingly parsed by a sort of exception to the foregoing rule—or rather, to that general rule of concord which the grammarians apply to the verb and its nominative. This construction is translated into English, and other modern tongues, sometimes literally, or nearly so, but much oftener, by a nominative and a finite verb. Example: "*[Greek: Eipen auton phonœthœnai]*."—*Mark*, x, 49. "Ait illum vocari."—*Leusden.* "Jussit eum vocari."—*Beza.* "Præcepit illum vocari."—*Vulgate.* "He commanded him to be called."—*English Bible.* "He commanded that he should be called."—*Milnes's Gr. Gram.*, p. 143. "Il dit qu'on l'appelât."—*French Bible.* "He bid that somebody should call him." "Il commanda qu'on le fît venir."—*Nouveau Test.*, Paris, 1812. "He commanded that they should *make him come*;" that is, "*lead him,* or *bring him.*" "Il commanda qu'on l'appelât."—*De Sacy's N. Test.*

OBS. 8.—In English, the objective case before the infinitive mood, although it may truly denote the agent of the infinitive action, or the subject of the infinitive passion, is nevertheless taken as the object of the preceding verb, participle, or preposition. Accordingly our language does not admit a literal translation of the above-mentioned construction, except the preceding verb be such as can be interpreted transitively. "*Gaudeo te val=ere,*" "I am glad that thou art well," cannot be translated more literally; because, "I am glad thee to be well," would not be good English. "*Aiunt regem advent=are,*" "They say the king is coming," may be otherwise rendered "They *declare* the king to be coming;" but neither version is entirely literal;

the objective being retained only by a change of *aiunt, say*, into such a verb as will govern the noun.

OBS. 9.—The following sentence is a literal imitation of the Latin accusative before the infinitive, and for that reason it is not good English: "But experience teacheth us, *both these opinions to be* alike ridiculous."—*Barclay's Works*, Vol. i, p. 262. It should be, "But experience *teaches us, that both these opinions are* alike ridiculous." The verbs *believe, think, imagine,* and others expressing *mental action,* I suppose to be capable of governing nouns or pronouns in the objective case, and consequently of being interpreted transitively. Hence I deny the correctness of the following explanation: "RULE XXIV. The objective case precedes the infinitive mode; [as,] 'I *believe* your *brother to be* a good man.' Here *believe* does not govern brother, in the objective case, because it is not the object after it. *Brother,* in the objective case, third person singular, precedes the neuter verb *to be,* in the infinitive mode, present time, third person singular."—*S. Barrett's Gram.*, p. 135. This author teaches that, "The *infinitive mode agrees* with the objective case in number and person."—*Ibid.* Which doctrine is denied; because the infinitive has no number or person, in any language. Nor do I see why the noun *brother,* in the foregoing example, may not be both the object of the active verb *believe,* and the subject of the neuter infinitive *to be,* at the same time; for the subject of the infinitive, if the infinitive can be said to have a subject, is not necessarily in the nominative case, or necessarily independent of what precedes.

OBS. 10.—There are many teachers of English grammar, who still adhere to the principle of the Latin and Greek grammarians, which refers the accusative or objective to the latter verb, and supposes the former to be intransitive, or to govern only the infinitive. Thus Nixon: "The objective case is frequently put before the infinitive mood, as its subject; as, 'Suffer *me* to depart.'" [340]—*English Parser*, p. 34. "When an objective case stands before an infinitive mood, as 'I understood *it* to be him,' 'Suffer *me* to depart,' such objective should be parsed, not as governed by the preceding verb, but as the objective case before the infinitive; that is, *the subject* of it. The reason of this is—the former verb can govern one object only, and that is (in such sentences) the infinitive mood; the intervening objective being the subject of the infinitive following, and not governed by the former verb; as, in that instance, it *would be governing* two objects."—*Ib., Note.*[341]

OBS. 11.—The notion that one verb governs an other in the infinitive, just as a transitive verb governs a noun, and so that it cannot also govern an objective case, is not only contradictory to my scheme of parsing the infinitive mood, but is also false in itself, and repugnant to the principles of General Grammar. In Greek and Latin, it is certainly no uncommon thing for a verb to govern two cases at once; and even the accusative before the infinitive is sometimes governed by the preceding verb, as the objective before the infinitive naturally is in English. But, in regard to construction, every language differs more or less from every other; hence each must have its own syntax, and abide by its own rules. In regard to the point here in question, the reader may compare the following examples: "[Greek: Echo anagkæn exelthein]."—*Luke,* xiv, 18. "Habeo necesse exire."—*Leusden.* English: "I have *occasion to go* away." Again: "[Greek: O echon hota akouein, akoueto]."—*Luke,* xiv, 35. "Habens aures audiendi, audiat."—*Leusden.* "Qui habet aures ad audiendum, audiat."—*Beza.* English: "He that hath *ears to hear,* let *him hear.*" But our most frequent use of the infinitive after the objective, is in sentences that must not be similarly constructed in Latin or Greek;[342] as, "And he commanded the *porter to watch.*"—*Mark,* xiii, 34. "And he delivered *Jesus to be crucified.*"—*Mark,* xv, 15. "And they led *him* out *to crucify him.*"—*Mark,* xv, 20. "We heard *him say.*"—*Mark,* xiv, 58. "That I might make *thee know.*"—*Prov.,* xxii, 21.

OBS. 12.—If our language does really admit any thing like the accusative before the infinitive, in the sense of a positive subject at the head of a clause, it is only in some prospective descriptions like the following: "Let certain studies be prescribed to be pursued during the freshman year; *some* of these to be attended to by the whole class; with regard to others, a *choice* to be allowed; *which*, when made by the student, (the parent or guardian sanctioning it,) to be binding during the freshman year: the same *plan* to be adopted with regard to the studies of the succeeding years."—GALLAUDET: *Journal of the N. Y. Literary Convention*, p. 118. Here the four words, *some, choice, which*, and *plan*, may appear to a Latinist to be so many objectives, or accusatives, placed before infinitives, and used to describe that state of things which the author would promote. If objectives they are, we may still suppose them to be governed by *let, would have,* or something of the kind, understood: as, "*Let* some of these be attended to;" or, "Some of these *I would have* to be attended to," &c. The relative *which* might with more propriety be made nominative, by changing "*to* be binding" to "*shall* be binding;" and as to the rest, it is very doubtful whether they are not now nominatives, rather than objectives. The infinitive, as used above, is a mere substitute for the Latin future participle; and any English noun or pronoun put absolute with a participle, is in the nominative case. English relatives are rarely, if ever, put absolute in this manner: and this may be the reason why the construction of *which*, in the sentence above, seems awkward. Besides, it is certain that the other pronouns are sometimes put absolute with the infinitive; and that, in the nominative case, not the objective: as,

"And *I to be* a corporal in his field,
And wear his colours like a tumbler's hoop!
What? *I! I love! I sue! I seek* a wife!"—Shak., *Love's Labour Lost*.

IMPROPRIETIES FOR CORRECTION.

FALSE SYNTAX UNDER RULE II.

THE SUBJECT OF A FINITE VERB.

"The whole need not a physician, but them that are sick."—*Bunyan's Law and Gr.*, p. iv.

[FORMULE.—Not proper, because the objective pronoun *them* is here made the subject of the verb *need*, understood. But, according to Rule 2d, "A noun or a pronoun which is the subject of a finite verb, must be in the nominative case." Therefore, *them* should be *they*; thus, "The whole need not a physician, but they that are sick."]

"He will in no wise cast out whomsoever cometh unto him."—*Robert Hall* "He feared the enemy might fall upon his men, whom he saw were off their guard."—*Hutchinson's Massachusetts*, ii, 133. "Whomsoever shall compel thee to go a mile, go with him twain."—*Dymond's Essays*, p. 48. "The idea's of the author have been conversant with the faults of other writers."—*Swift's T. T.*, p. 55. "You are a much greater loser than me by his death."—*Swift to Pope*, l. 63. "Such peccadillo's pass with him for pious frauds."—*Barclay's Works*, Vol. iii, p. 279. "In whom I am nearly concerned, and whom I know would be very apt to justify my whole procedure."—*Ib.*, i, 560. "Do not think such a man as me contemptible for my garb."—*Addison*. "His wealth and him bid adieu to each other."—*Priestley's Gram.*, p. 107. "So that, 'He is greater than *me*,' will be more grammatical than, 'He is greater than *I*.'"—*Ib.*, p. 106. "The Jesuits had more interests at court than him."—SMOLLETT: in *Pr. Gram.*, p. 106.[343] "Tell the Cardinal that I understand poetry better than him."—*Id., ib.* "An inhabitant of Crim Tartary was far more happy than him."—*Id., ib.* "My father and him have been very intimate since."—*Fair American*, ii, 53.

"Who was the agent, and whom the object struck or kissed?"—*Infant School Gram.*, p. 32. "To find the person whom he imagined was concealed there."—*Kirkham's Elocution,* p. 225. "He offered a great recompense to whomsoever would help him."—HUME: in *Pr. Gram.*, p. 104. "They would be under the dominion, absolute and unlimited, of whomsoever might exercise the right of judgement."—*Gov. Haynes's Speech*, in 1832. "They had promised to accept whomsoever should be born in Wales."—*Stories by Croker.* "We sorrow not as them that have no hope."—*Maturin's Sermons,* p. 27. "If he suffers, he suffers as them that have no hope."—*Ib.*, p. 32. "We acknowledge that he, and him only, hath been our peacemaker."—*Gratton.* "And what can be better than him that made it?"—*Jenks's Prayers*, p. 329. "None of his school-fellows is more beloved than him."—*Cooper's Gram.*, p. 42. "Solomon, who was wiser than them all."—*Watson's Apology*, p. 76. "Those whom the Jews thought were the last to be saved, first entered the kingdom of God."—*Eleventh Hour, Tract,* No. 4. "A stone is heavy, and the sand weighty; but a fool's wrath is heavier than them both."—*Prov.,* xxvii, 3. "A man of business, in good company, is hardly more insupportable than her they call a notable woman."—*Steele, Sped.* "The king of the Sarmatians, whom we may imagine was no small prince, restored him a hundred thousand Roman prisoners."—*Life of Antoninus*, p. 83. "Such notions would be avowed at this time by none but rosicrucians, and fanatics as mad as them."—*Bolingbroke's Ph. Tr.*, p. 24. "Unless, as I said, Messieurs, you are the masters, and not me."—BASIL HALL: *Harrison's E. Lang.*, p. 173. "We had drawn up against peaceable travellers, who must have been as glad as us to escape."—BURNES'S TRAVELS: *ibid.* "Stimulated, in turn, by their approbation, and that of better judges than them, she turned to their literature with redoubled energy."—QUARTERLY REVIEW: *Life of H. More: ibid.* "I know not whom else are expected."—SCOTT'S PIRATE: *ibid.* "He is great, but truth is greater than us all."—*Horace Mann, in*

Congress, 1850. "Him I accuse has entered."—*Fowler's E. Gram.*, §482: see *Shakspeare's Coriolanus*, Act V, sc. 5.

"Scotland and thee did each in other live."
—*Dryden's Po.*, Vol. ii, p. 220.

"We are alone; here's none but thee and I."
—*Shak.*, 2 Hen. VI.

"Me rather had, my heart might feel your love,
Than my unpleas'd eye see your courtesy."
—*Idem: Joh. Dict.*

"Tell me, in sadness, whom is she you love?"
—*Id., Romeo and Juliet*, A. I, sc. 1.

"Better leave undone, than by our deeds acquire
Too high a fame, when him we serve's away."
—*Shak., Ant. and Cleop.*

RULE III.—APPOSITION.

A Noun or a personal Pronoun used to explain a preceding noun or pronoun, is put, by apposition, in the same case: as, "But it is really *I*, your old *friend and neighbour., Piso*, late a *dweller* upon the Coelian hill, who am now basking in the warm skies of Palmyra."—*Zenobia*.

"But *he*, our gracious *Master*, kind as just,
Knowing our frame, remembers we are dust."—*Barbauld*.

OBSERVATIONS ON RULE III.

OBS. 1—*Apposition* is that peculiar relation which one noun or pronoun bears to an other, when two or more are placed together in the same case, and used to designate the same person or thing: as, "*Cicero* the *orator*;"—"The *prophet Joel*;"—"*He* of Gath, *Goliah*;"—"Which *ye yourselves* do know;"—"To make *him king*;"—"To give his *life* a *ransom* for many;"—"I made the *ground* my *bed*;"—"*I*, thy *schoolmaster*;"—"*We* the *People* of the United States." This placing-together of nouns and pronouns in the same case, was reckoned by the old grammarians a *figure of syntax*; and from them it received, in their elaborate detail of the grammatical and rhetorical figures, its present name of *apposition*. They reckoned it a species of *ellipsis,* and supplied between the words, the participle *being,* the infinitive *to be,* or some other part of their "*substantive verb*:" as, "Cicero *being* the orator;"—"To make him *to be* king;"—"I *who am* thy schoolmaster." But the later Latin grammarians have usually placed it among their regular concords; some calling it the first concord, while others make it the last, in the series; and some, with no great regard to consistency, treating it both as a figure and as a regular concord, at the same time.

OBS. 2.—Some English grammarians teach, "that the words in the cases preceding and following the verb *to be*, may be said to be *in apposition* to each other."—*Murray's Gram.*, 8vo, p. 181; *R. C. Smith's*, 155; *Fisk's*, 126; *Ingersoll's*, 146; *Merchant's*, 91. But this is entirely repugnant to the doctrine, that apposition is a *figure*; nor is it at all consistent with the original meaning of the word *apposition*; because it assumes that the literal reading, when the supposed ellipsis is supplied, is *apposition* still. The old distinction, however, between apposition and same cases, is *generally* preserved in our grammars, and is worthy ever to be so. The rule for *same cases* applies to all nouns or pronouns that are put after verbs or participles not transitive, and that are made to agree in case with other nouns or pronouns going before, and meaning the same thing. But some teachers who observe this distinction with reference to the neuter verb *be,* and to certain passive verbs of *naming, appointing,* and the like, absurdly break it down in relation to other verbs, neuter or active-intransitive. Thus Nixon: "Nouns in apposition are in the same case; as, '*Hortensius* died a *martyr*;' '*Sydney* lived the shepherd's *friend.*'"—*English Parser,* p. 55. It is remarkable that *all* this author's examples of "*nominatives in apposition,*" (and he gives eighteen in the exercise,) are precisely of this sort, in which there is really *no apposition at all.*

OBS. 3.—In the exercise of parsing, rule third should be applied only to the *explanatory term*; because the case of the *principal term* depends on its relation to the rest of the sentence, and comes under some other rule. In certain instances, too, it is better to waive the analysis which *might* be made under rule third, and to take both or all the terms together, under the rule for the main relation. Thus, the several proper names which distinguish an individual, are always in apposition, and should be taken together in parsing; as, *William Pitt—Marcus Tullius Cicero.* It may, I think, be proper to include with the personal names, some titles also; as, *Lord Bacon—Sir Isaac Newton.* William E. Russell and Jonathan Ware, (two American authors of no great note,) in parsing the name of "*George Washington,*" absurdly take the former word as an *adjective* belonging to the latter. See *Russell's Gram.,* p. 100; and *Ware's,* 17. R. C. Smith does the same, both with honorary titles, and with baptismal or Christian names. See his *New Gram.,* p. 97. And one English writer, in explaining the phrases, "*John Wickliffe's influence,*" "*Robert Bruce's exertions,*" and the like, will have the first nouns to be governed by the last, and the intermediate ones to be distinct possessives *in apposition* with the former. See *Nixon's English Parser,* p. 59. Wm. B. Fowle, in his "True English Grammar," takes all titles, all given names, all possessives, and all pronouns, to be adjectives. According to him, this class embraces more than half the words in the language. A later writer than any of these says, "The proper noun is *philosophically* an adjective. Nouns common or proper, of similar or dissimilar import, *may be parsed as adjectives*, when they become qualifying or distinguishing words; as, *President* Madison,—*Doctor* Johnson,—*Mr.* Webster,—*Esq.* Carleton,—*Miss* Gould,—*Professor* Ware,—*lake* Erie,—the *Pacific* ocean,—*Franklin* House,—*Union* street."—*Sanborn's Gram.*, p. 134. I dissent from all these views, at least so far as not to divide a *man's name* in parsing it. A person will sometimes have such a multitude of names, that it would be a flagrant waste of time, to parse them all separately: for example, that wonderful doctor, *Paracelsus*, who called himself, "Aureolus Philippus Theophrastus Bombastus Paracelsus de Hoenheim."—*Univ. Biog. Dict.*

OBS. 4.—A very common rule for apposition in Latin, is this: "Substantives signifying the same thing, agree in case."—*Adam's Latin Gram.*, p. 156. The same has also been applied to our language: "Substantives denoting the same person or thing, agree in case."—*Bullions's E. Gram.*, p. 102. This rule is, for two reasons, very faulty: first, because the apposition of *pronouns* seems not to be included it; secondly, because two nouns that are not in the same case, do sometimes "signify" or "denote" the same thing. Thus, "*the city of London*," means only *the city London*; "*the land of Egypt*," is only Egypt; and "*the person of Richard*" is *Richard himself.* Dr. Webster defines *apposition* to be, "The placing of two nouns in the same case, without a connecting word between them."—*Octavo Dict.* This, too, excludes the pronouns, and has exceptions, both various and numerous. In the first place, the apposition may be of more than two nouns, without any connective; as, "*Ezra* the *priest*, the *scribe* of the law."—*Ezra*, vii, 21. Secondly, two nouns connected by a conjunction, may both be put in apposition with a preceding noun or pronoun; as, "God hath made that same *Jesus*, whom ye have crucified, both *Lord* and *Christ*."—*Acts*, ii, 36. "Who made *me* a *judge* or a *divider* over you."—*Luke*, xii, 14. Thirdly, the apposition may be of two nouns immediately connected by *and*, provided the two words denote but one person or thing; as, "This great *philosopher and statesman* was bred a printer." Fourthly, it may be of two words connected by *as*, expressing the idea of a partial or assumed identity; as, "Yet count *him* not *as* an *enemy*, but admonish *him as* a *brother*."—*2 Thess.*, iii, 15. "So that *he, as God*, sitteth in the temple of God."—*Ib.*, ii, 4. Fifthly, it may perhaps be of two words connected by *than*; as, "He left *them* no more *than* dead *men*."—*Law and Grace*, p. 28. Lastly, there is a near resemblance to apposition, when two equivalent nouns are connected by *or*; as, "The back of the hedgehog is covered with *prickles, or spines*."—*Webster's Dict.*

OBS. 5.—To the rule for apposition, as I have expressed it, there are properly *no exceptions*. But there are many puzzling examples of construction under it, some of which are but little short of exceptions; and upon such of these as are most likely to embarrass the learner, some further observations shall be made. The rule supposes the first word to be the principal term, with which the other word, or subsequent noun or pronoun, is in apposition; and it generally is so: but the explanatory word is sometimes placed first, especially among the poets; as,

"From bright'ning fields of ether fair disclos'd, *Child* of the sun, refulgent *Summer* comes."—*Thomson.*

OBS. 6.—The pronouns of the *first* and *second* persons are often placed before nouns merely to distinguish their person; as, "*I John* saw these things."—*Bible.* "But what is this to *you receivers?*"—*Clarkson's Essay on Slavery*, p. 108. "His praise, *ye brooks*, attune."—*Thomson.* In this case of apposition, the words are in general closely united, and either of them may be taken as the explanatory term. The learner will find it easier to parse *the noun* by rule third; or *both nouns*, if there be two: as, "*I* thy *father-in-law Jethro* am come unto thee."—*Exod.*, xviii, 6. There are many other examples, in which it is of no moment, which of the terms we take for the principal; and to all such the rule may be applied literally: as, "Thy *son Benhadad king* of Syria hath sent me to thee."—*2 Kings*, viii, 9.

OBS. 7.—When two or more nouns of the *possessive case* are put in apposition, the possessive termination added to one, denotes the case of both or all; as, "For *Herodias*' sake, his *brother Philip's wife*"—*Matt.*, xiv, 3; Mark, vi, 17. Here *wife* is in apposition with *Herodias*', and *brother* with *Philip's*; consequently all these words are reckoned to be in the possessive case. The Greek text, which is better, stands essentially thus: "For the sake of Herodias, the wife of Philip his brother." "For *Jacob* my *servant's* sake, and *Israel* mine *elect*."—*Isaiah*, xlv, 4. Here, as *Jacob* and *Israel* are only different names for the same person or nation, the four nouns in Italics are, according to the rule, all made possessives by the one sign used; but the construction is not to be commended: it would be better to say, "For *the* sake *of* Jacob my servant, and Israel mine elect." "With *Hyrcanus* the high *priest's* consent."—*Wood's Dict., w. Herod.* "I called at *Smith's*, the *bookseller*; or, at *Smith* the *bookseller's*."— *Bullions's E. Gram.*, p. 105. Two words, each having the possessive sign, can never be in apposition one with the other; because that sign has immediate reference to the governing noun expressed or understood after it; and if it be repeated, separate governing nouns will be implied, and the apposition will be destroyed.[344]

OBS. 8.—If the foregoing remark is just, the apposition of two nouns in the possessive case, requires the possessive sign to be added to that noun which immediately precedes the governing word, whether expressed or understood, and positively excludes it from the other. The sign of the case is added, sometimes to the former, and sometimes to the latter noun, but never to both: or, if added to both, the two words are no longer in apposition. Example: "And for that reason they ascribe to him a great part of his *father Nimrod's*, or *Belus's* actions."—*Rollin's An. Hist.*, Vol. ii, p. 6. Here *father* and *Nimrod's* are in strict apposition; but if *actions* governs *Belus's*, the same word is implied to govern *Nimrod's*, and the two names are not in apposition, though they are in the same case and mean the same person.

OBS. 9.—Dr. Priestley says, "Some would say, 'I left the parcel at *Mr. Smith's*, the *bookseller*;' others, 'at *Mr. Smith* the *bookseller's*;' and perhaps others, at '*Mr. Smith's* the *bookseller's*.' The last of these forms is most agreeable to the Latin idiom, but the first seems to be more natural in ours; and if the addition consist [*consists*, says Murray,] of two or more words, *the case seems to be very clear*; as, 'I left the parcel at *Mr. Smith's* the *bookseller* and *stationer*;' i. e. at Mr. Smith's, *who is a* bookseller and stationer."—*Priestley's Gram.*, p. 70. Here the examples, if rightly pointed, *would all be right*; but the ellipsis supposed, not only destroys the apposition, but converts the explanatory noun into a nominative. And in the phrase, "at *Mr. Smiths, the bookseller's*," there is no apposition, except that of *Mr.* with *Smith's*; for the governing noun *house* or *store* is understood as clearly after the one possessive sign as after the other. Churchill imagines that in Murray's example, "I reside at *Lord Stormont's*, my old *patron* and *benefactor*," the last two nouns are in the nominative after "*who was*" understood; and also erroneously suggests, that their joint apposition with *Stormont's* might be secured, by saying, less elegantly, "I reside at Lord *Stormont's*, my old patron and *benefactor's*."— *Churchill's New Gram.*, p. 285. Lindley Murray, who tacitly takes from Priestley all that is quoted above, except the term "*Mr.*," and the notion of an ellipsis of "*who is*," assumes each of the three forms as an instance of apposition, but pronounces the first only to be "correct and proper." If, then, the first is elliptical, as Priestley suggests, and the others are ungrammatical, as Murray pretends to prove, we cannot have in reality any such construction as the apposition of two possessives; for the sign of the case cannot possibly be added in more than these three ways. But Murray does not adhere at all to his own decision, as may be seen by his subsequent remarks and examples, on the same page; as, "The *emperor Leopold's*;"—"*Dionysius* the *tyrant's*;"—"For *David* my *servant's* sake;"—"Give me here *John* the *Baptist's* head;"—"*Paul* the *apostle's* advice." See *Murray's Gram.*, 8vo, p. 176; *Smith's New Gram.*, p. 150; and others.

OBS. 10.—An explanatory noun without the possessive sign, seems sometimes to be put in apposition with a *pronoun of the possessive case*; and, if introduced by the conjunction *as*, it may either precede or follow the pronoun: thus, "I rejoice in *your* success *as* an *instructer*."— *Sanborn's Gram.*, p. 244. "*As* an *author*, his 'Adventurer' is *his* capital work."— *Murray's Sequel*, p. 329.

"Thus shall mankind *his* guardian care engage,
The promised *father* of a future age."—*Pope*.

But possibly such examples may be otherwise explained on the principle of ellipsis; as, [*He being*] "the promised *father*," &c. "As [*he was*] an *author*," &c. "As [*you are*] an *instructer*."

OBS. 11.—When a noun or pronoun *is repeated* for the sake of emphasis, or for the adding of an epithet, the word which is repeated may properly be said to be in apposition with that which is first introduced; or, if not, the repetition itself implies sameness of case: as, "They have forsaken *me*, the *fountain* of living waters, and hewed them out *cisterns*, broken *cisterns*, that can hold no water."—*Jer.*, ii, 13.

"I find the total of their hopes and fears *Dreams*, empty *dreams*."— *Cowper's Task*, p. 71.

OBS. 12.—A noun is sometimes put, as it were, in apposition to a *sentence*; being used (perhaps elliptically) to sum up the whole idea in one emphatic word, or short phrase. But, in such instances, the noun can seldom be said to have any positive relation that may determine its case; and, if alone, it will of course be in the nominative, by reason of its independence. Examples: "He permitted me to consult his library—a *kindness* which I shall not forget."—*W. Allen's Gram.*, p. 148. "I have offended reputation—a most unnoble *swerving*."—*Shakspeare*. "I want a hero,—an uncommon *want*."—*Byron*. "Lopez took up the sonnet, and after reading it several times, frankly acknowledged that he did not understand it himself; a *discovery* which the poet probably never made before."—*Campbell's Rhet.*, p. 280.

"In Christian hearts O for a pagan zeal!
A needful, but opprobrious *prayer!*"—*Young*, N. ix, l. 995.

"Great standing *miracle*, that Heav'n assign'd
Its only thinking thing this turn of mind."—*Pope*.

OBS. 13.—A *distributive term* in the singular number, is frequently construed in apposition with a comprehensive plural; as, "*They* reap vanity, *every one* with his neighbour."—*Bible*. "Go *ye every man* unto his city."—*Ibid*. So likewise with two or more singular nouns which are taken conjointly; as, "The *Son and Spirit* have *each* his proper office."—*Butler's Analogy*, p. 163. And sometimes a *plural* word is emphatically put after a series of particulars comprehended under it; as, "Ambition, interest, glory, *all* concurred."—*Letters on Chivalry*, p. 11. "Royalists, republicans, churchmen, sectaries, courtiers, patriots, *all parties* concurred in the illusion."—*Hume's History*, Vol. viii, p. 73. The foregoing examples are plain, but similar expressions sometimes require care, lest the distributive or collective term be so placed that its construction and meaning may be misapprehended. Examples: "We have *turned every one* to his own way."—*Isaiah*, liii, 6. Better: "*We have every one* turned to his own way." "For in many things we *offend all*."—*James*, iii, 2. Better: "For in many things *we all* offend." The latter readings doubtless convey the *true sense* of these texts. To the relation of apposition, it may be proper also to refer the construction of a singular noun taken in a distributive sense and repeated after *by* to denote order; as, "*They* went out *one* by one."—*Bible.* "Our whole *company, man* by man, ventured in."—*Goldsmith.* "To examine a *book, page* by page; to search a *place, house* by house."—*Ward's Gram.*, p. 106. So too, perhaps, when the parts of a thing explain the whole; as,

"But those that sleep, and think not on their sins,
Pinch *them, arms, legs, backs, shoulders, sides,* and *shins.*"
—*Shak.*

OBS. 14.—To express a reciprocal action or relation, the pronominal adjectives *each other* and *one an other* are employed: as, "They love *each other*;"—"They love *one an other.*" The words, separately considered, are singular; but, taken together, they imply plurality; and they can be properly construed only after plurals, or singulars taken conjointly. *Each other* is usually applied to two persons or things; and *one an other,* to more than two. The impropriety of applying them otherwise, is noticed elsewhere; (see, in Part II, Obs. 15th, on the Classes of Adjectives;) so that we have here to examine only their relations of case. The terms, though reciprocal and closely united, are seldom or never in the same construction. If such expressions be analyzed, *each* and *one* will generally appear to be in the nominative case, and *other* in the objective; as, "They love *each other*;" i. e. *each* loves *the other.* "They love *one an other*;" i. e. any or every *one* loves any or every *other. Each* and *one* (—if the words be taken as cases, and not adjectively—) are properly in agreement or apposition with *they,* and *other* is governed by the verb. The terms, however, admit of other constructions; as, "Be ye helpers *one* of an *other.*"—*Bible.* Here *one* is in apposition with *ye,* and *other* is governed by *of.* "Ye are *one* an *other's* joy."—*Ib.* Here *one* is in apposition with *ye,* and *other's* is in the possessive case, being governed by *joy*. "Love will make you *one* an *other's* joy." Here *one* is in the objective case, being in apposition with *you*, and *other's* is governed as before. "*Men's* confidence in *one an other*;"—"*Their* dependence *one* upon *an other*." Here the word *one* appears to be in apposition with the possessive going before; for it has already been shown, that words standing in that relation *never take the possessive sign*. But if its location after the preposition must make it objective, the whole object is the complex term, "*one an other*." "Grudge not *one* against *an other*."—*James*, v, 9. "Ne vous plaignez point *les uns des autres*."—*French Bible.* "Ne suspirate *alius* adversus *alium*."—*Beza.* "Ne ingemiscite adversus *alii alios.*"—*Leusden.* "[Greek: Mæ stenazete kat hallælon]."—*Greek New Testament.*

OBS. 15.—The construction of the Latin terms *alius alium, alii alios,* &c., with that of the French *l'un l'autre, l'un de l'autre,* &c., appears, at first view, sufficiently to confirm the doctrine of the preceding observation; but, besides the frequent use, in Latin and Greek, of a reciprocal adverb to express the meaning of one an other or each other, there are, from each of these languages, some analogical arguments for taking the English terms together as compounds. The most common term in Greek for *one an other,* ([Greek: Hallælon], dat. [Greek: hallælois, ais, ois], acc. [Greek: hallælous]: ab [Greek: hallos], *alius,*) is a single derivative word, the case of which is known by its termination; and *each other* is sometimes expressed in Latin by a compound: as, "Et osculantes se *alterutrum*, fleverunt pariter."—*Vulgate.* That is: "And kissing *each other*, they wept together." As this text speaks of but two persons, our translators have not expressed it well in the common version: "And they kissed *one an other*, and wept *one* with *an other*"—*1 Sam.*, xx, 41. *Alter-utrum* is composed of a nominative and an accusative, like *each-other*; and, in the nature of things, there is no reason why the former should be compounded, and the latter not. Ordinarily, there seems to be no need of compounding either of them. But some examples occur, in which it is not easy to parse *each other* and *one an other* otherwise than as compounds: as, "He only recommended this, and not the washing of *one another's* feet."—*Barclay's Works*, Vol. iii, p. 143.

"The Temple late two brother sergeants saw,
Who deem'd *each other oracles* of law."—*Pope*, B. ii, Ep. 2.[345]

OBS. 16.—The *common* and the *proper* name of an object are very often associated, and put in apposition; as, "*The river Thames*,"—"*The ship Albion*,"—"*The poet Cowper*"—"*Lake Erie*,"—"*Cape May*"—"*Mount Atlas*." But, in English, the proper name of a place, when accompanied by the common name, is generally put in the objective case, and preceded by *of*; as, "The city *of* New York,"—"The land *of* Canaan,"—"The island *of* Cuba,"—"The peninsula *of* Yucatan." Yet in some instances, even of this kind, the immediate apposition is preferred; as, "That the *city Sepphoris* should be subordinate to the *city Tiberias*."—*Life of Josephus*, p. 142. In the following sentence, the preposition *of* is at least needless: "The law delighteth herself in the number *of* twelve; and the number *of* twelve is much respected in holy writ."—*Coke, on Juries*. Two or three late grammarians, supposing *of* always to indicate a possessive relation between one thing and an other, contend that it is no less improper, to say, "The city *of* London, the city *of* New Haven, the month *of* March, the islands *of* Cuba and Hispaniola, the towns *of* Exeter and Dover," than to say, "King *of* Solomon, Titus *of* the Roman Emperor, Paul *of* the apostle, or, Cicero *of* the orator."—See *Barrett's Gram.*, p. 101; *Emmons's*, 16. I cannot but think there is some mistake in their mode of finding out what is proper or improper in grammar. Emmons scarcely achieved two pages more, before he forgot his criticism, and adopted the phrase, "in the city *of* New Haven."—*Gram.*, p. 19.

OBS. 17.—When an object acquires a new name or character from the action of a verb, the new appellation is put in apposition with the object of the active verb, and in the nominative after the passive: as, "They named the *child John*;"—"The child was named *John*."—"They elected *him president*;"—"He was elected *president*." After the active verb, the acquired name must be parsed by Rule 3d; after the passive, by Rule 6th. In the following example, the pronominal adjective *some*, or the noun *men* understood after it, is the direct object of the verb *gave*, and the nouns expressed are in apposition with it: "And he gave *some, apostles*; and *some, prophets*; and *some, evangelists*; and *some, pastors* and *teachers*"—*Ephesians*, iv, 11. That is, "He *bestowed some* [men] as *apostles*; and *some* as *prophets*; and *some* as *evangelists*; and *some* as *pastors* and *teachers*." The common reader might easily mistake the meaning and construction of this text in two different ways; for he might take *some* to be either a *dative case*, meaning *to some persons*, or an adjective to the nouns which are here expressed. The punctuation, however, is calculated to show that the nouns are in apposition with *some*, or *some men*, in what the Latins call the *accusative, case*. But the version ought to be amended by the insertion of *as*, which would here be an express sign of the apposition intended.

OBS. 18.—Some authors teach that words in apposition must agree in person, number, and gender, as well as in case; but such agreement the following examples show not to be always necessary: "The *Franks, a people* of Germany."—*W. Allen's Gram*. "The Kenite *tribe*, the *descendants* of Hobab."—*Milman's Hist. of the Jews*. "But how can *you* a *soul*, still either hunger or thirst?"—*Lucian's Dialogues*, p. 14. "Who seized the wife of *me* his *host*, and fled."—*Ib.*, p. 16.

"Thy gloomy *grandeurs* (Nature's most august.
Inspiring *aspect*!) claim a grateful verse."—*Young*, N. ix, l. 566.

IMPROPRIETIES FOR CORRECTION.

FALSE SYNTAX UNDER RULE III.

ERRORS OF WORDS IN APPOSITION.

"Now, therefore, come thou, let us make a covenant, I and thou."—*Gen.*, xxxi, 44.

[FORMULE.—Not proper, because the pronouns I and thou, of the nominative case, are here put in apposition with the preceding pronoun *us*, which is objective. But, according to Rule 3d, "A noun or a personal pronoun, used to explain a preceding noun or pronoun, is put, by apposition, in the same case." Therefore, *I* and *thou* should be *thee* and *me*; (the first person, in our idiom, being usually put last;) thus, "Now, therefore, come thou, let us make a covenant, thee and me."]

"Now, therefore, come thou, we will make a covenant, thee and me."—*Variation of Gen.* "The word came not to Esau, the hunter, that stayed not at home; but to Jacob, the plain man, he that dwelt in tents."—*Wm. Penn.* "Not to every man, but to the man of God, (i. e.) he that is led by the spirit of God."—*Barclays Works*, i, 266. "For, admitting God to be a creditor, or he to whom the debt should be paid, and Christ he that satisfies or pays it on behalf of man the debtor, this question will arise, whether he paid that debt as God, or man, or both?"—*Wm. Penn.* "This Lord Jesus Christ, the heavenly Man, the Emmanuel, God with us, we own and believe in: he whom the high priests raged against," &c.—*George Fox.* "Christ, and Him crucified, was the Alpha and Omega of all his addresses, the fountain and foundation of his hope and trust."—*Experience of Paul*, p. 399. "'Christ and Him crucified' is the head, and only head, of the church."—*Denison's Sermon.* "But if 'Christ and Him crucified' are the burden of the ministry, such disastrous results are all avoided."—*Ib.* "He never let fall the least intimation, that himself, or any other person, whomsoever, was the object of worship."—*Hannah Adams's View*, p. 250. "Let the elders that rule well, be counted worthy of double honour, especially they who labour in the word and doctrine."—*1 Tim.*, v, 17. "Our Shepherd, him who is styled King of saints, will assuredly give his saints the victory."—*Sermon*. "It may seem odd to talk of *we subscribers*"—*Fowlers True Eng. Gram.*, p. 20. "And they shall have none to bury them, them, their wives, nor their sons, nor their daughters; for I will pour their wickedness upon them."—*Jeremiah*, xiv, 16. "Yet I supposed it necessary to send to you Epaphroditus, my brother, and companion in labour, and fellow-soldier, but your messenger, and he that ministered to my wants."—*Philippians*, ii, 25.

"Amidst the tumult of the routed train,
The sons of false Antimachus were slain;
He, who for bribes his faithless counsels sold,
And voted Helen's stay for Paris' gold."
—*Pope, Iliad*, B. xi. l. 161.

"See the vile King his iron sceptre bear—
His only praise attends the pious Heir;
He, in whose soul the virtues all conspire,
The best good son, from the worst wicked sire."
—DR. LOWTH: *Union Poems*, p. 19.

"Then from thy lips poured forth a joyful song
To thy Redeemer!—yea, it poured along
In most melodious energy of praise,
To God, the Saviour, he of ancient days."
—*Arm Chair*, p. 15.

RULE IV.—POSSESSIVES.

A Noun or a Pronoun in the possessive case, is governed by the name of the thing possessed: as, "*God's* mercy prolongs *man's* life."—*Allen*.

> "*Theirs* is the vanity, the learning *thine*; Touched by *thy* hand, again *Rome's* glories shine."—*Pope*.

OBSERVATIONS ON RULE IV.

OBS. 1.—Though the *ordinary* syntax of the possessive case is sufficiently plain and easy, there is perhaps, among all the puzzling and disputable points of grammar, nothing more difficult of decision, than are some questions that occur respecting the right management of this case. That its usual construction is both clearly and properly stated in the foregoing rule, is what none will doubt or deny. But how many and what exceptions to this rule ought to be allowed, or whether any are justly demanded or not, are matters about which there may be much diversity of opinion. Having heretofore published the rule without any express exceptions, I am not now convinced that it is best to add any; yet are there three different modes of expression which might be plausibly exhibited in that character. Two of these would concern only the parser; and, for that reason, they seem not to be very important. The other involves the approval or reprehension of a great multitude of very common expressions, concerning which our ablest grammarians differ in opinion, and our most popular digest plainly contradicts itself. These points are; *first*, the apposition of possessives, and the supposed ellipses which may affect that construction; *secondly*, the government of the possessive case after *is, was*, &c., when the ownership of a thing is simply affirmed or denied; *thirdly*, the government of the possessive by a participle, as such—that is, while it retains the government and adjuncts of a participle.

OBS. 2.—The apposition of one possessive with an other, (as, "For *David* my *servant's* sake,") might doubtless be consistently made a formal exception to the direct government of the possessive by its controlling noun. But this apposition is only a sameness of construction, so that what governs the one, virtually governs the other. And if the case of any noun or pronoun is known and determined by the rule or relation of apposition, there can be no need of an exception to the foregoing rule for the purpose of parsing it, since that purpose is already answered by rule third. If the reader, by supposing an ellipsis which I should not, will resolve any given instance of this kind into something else than apposition, I have already shown him that some great grammarians have differed in the same way before. Useless ellipses, however, should never be supposed; and such *perhaps* is the following: "At Mr. Smith's [*who is*] the bookseller."—See *Dr. Priestley's Gram.*, p. 71.

OBS. 3.—In all our Latin grammars, the verb *sum, fui, esse*, to be, is said (though not with strict propriety) sometimes to *signify* possession, property, or duty, and in that sense to govern the genitive case: as, "*Est regis*;"—"It is the king's."—"*Hominis est errare*;"—"It is man's to err."—"*Pecus est Meliboeœi*;"—"The flock is Meliboeus's." And sometimes, with like import, this verb, expressed or understood, may govern the dative; as, "*Ego* [sum] *dilecto meo, et dilectus meus* [est] *mihi*."—*Vulgate.* "I am my beloved's, and my beloved is mine."—*Solomon's Song*, vi, 3. Here, as both the genitive and the dative are expressed in English by the possessive, if the former are governed by the verb, there seems to be precisely the same reason from the nature of the expression, and an additional one from analogy, for considering the latter to be so too. But all the annotators upon the Latin syntax suggest, that the genitive thus put after *sum* or *est*, is really governed, not by the verb, but by some *noun understood*; and with this idea, of an ellipsis in the construction, all our English grammarians appear to unite. They might not, however, find it very easy to tell by what noun the word *beloved's* or *mine* is governed, in the last example above; and so of many others, which are used in the same way: as, "There shall nothing die of all that is the *children's* of Israel."—*Exod.*, ix, 4. The Latin here is, "Ut nihil omnino pereat ex his *quæ pertinent ad* filios Israel."—*Vulgate*. That is, —"of all those *which belong to* the children of Israel."

"For thou art *Freedom's* now—and *Fame's*,
One of the few, the immortal names,
That were not born to die."—HALLECK: *Marco Bozzaris*.

OBS. 4.—Although the possessive case is always intrinsically an *adjunct* and therefore incapable of being used or comprehended in any sense that is positively abstract; yet we see that there are instances in which it is used with a certain degree of abstraction,—that is, with an actual separation from the name of the thing possessed; and that accordingly there are, in the simple personal pronouns, (where such a distinction is most needed,) two different forms of the case; the one adapted to the concrete, and the other to the abstract construction. That form of the pronoun, however, which is equivalent in sense to the concrete and the noun, is still the possessive case, and nothing more; as, "All *mine* are *thine*, and *thine* are *mine*."—*John*, xvii, 10. For if we suppose this equivalence to prove such a pronoun to be something more than the possessive case, as do some grammarians, we must suppose the same thing respecting the possessive case of a noun, whenever the relation of ownership or possession is simply affirmed or denied with such a noun put last: as, "For all things are *yours*; and ye are *Christ's*; and Christ is *God's*."—*1 Cor.*, iii, 21. By the second example placed under the rule, I meant to suggest, that the possessive case, when placed before or after this verb, (*be*,) *might* be parsed as being governed by the nominative; as we may suppose "*theirs*" to be governed by "*vanity*," and "*thine*" by "*learning*," these nouns being the names of the things possessed. But then we encounter a difficulty, whenever a *pronoun* happens to be the nominative; as, "Therefore glorify God in your body, and in your spirit, *which are God's*"—*1 Cor.*, vi, 20. Here the common resort would be to some ellipsis; and yet it must be confessed, that this mode of interpretation cannot but make some difference in the sense: as, "*If ye be Christ's*, then are ye Abraham's seed."—*Gal.*, iii, 29. Here some may think the meaning to be, "*If ye be Christ's seed*, or *children*." But a truer version of the text would be, "If ye *are of Christ*, then are ye Abraham's seed."—"Que si vous *êtes à Christ*, vous êtes donc la posterité d'Abraham."—*French Bible.*

OBS. 5.—Possession is the having of something, and if the possessive case is always an adjunct, referring either directly or indirectly to that which constitutes it a possessive, it would seem but reasonable, to limit the government of this case to that part of speech which is understood *substantively*—that is, to "the *name* of the thing possessed." Yet, in violation of this restriction, many grammarians admit, that a *participle*, with the regimen and adjuncts of a participle, may govern the possessive case; and some of them, at the same time, with astonishing inconsistency, aver, that the possessive case before a participle converts the latter into a noun, and necessarily deprives it of its regimen. Whether participles are worthy to form an exception to my rule or not, this palpable contradiction is one of the gravest faults of L. Murray's code of syntax. After copying from Lowth the doctrine that a participle with an *article* before it becomes a noun, and must drop the government and adjuncts of a participle, this author informs us, that the same principles are applicable to the *pronoun* and participle: as, "Much depends on *their observing of* the rule, and error will be the consequence of *their neglecting of* it;" in stead of, "*their observing the rule*," and "*their neglecting it*." And this doctrine he applies, with yet more positiveness, to the *noun* and participle; as if the error were still more glaring, to make an active participle govern a possessive *noun*; saying, "We shall perceive this *more clearly*, if we substitute a noun for the pronoun: as, 'Much depends upon *Tyro's observing of* the rule,' &c.; which is the same as, 'Much depends on Tyro's *observance* of the rule.' But, as this construction sounds rather *harshly*, it would, in general, be better to express the sentiment in the following, or some other form: 'Much depends on the *rule's being observed*; and error will be the consequence of *its being neglected*? or—'*on observing the rule*; and—*of neglecting it*.'"—*Murray's Gram.*, 8vo, p. 193; *Ingersoll's*, 199; and others.

OBS. 6.—Here it is assumed, that "*their observing the rule*," or "*Tyro's observing the rule*," is an ungrammatical phrase; and, several different methods being suggested for its correction, a preference is at length given to what is perhaps not less objectionable than the original phrase itself. The last form offered, "*on observing the rule*," &c., is indeed correct enough in itself; but, as a substitute for the other, it is both inaccurate and insufficient. It merely omits the possessive case, and leaves the action of the participle undetermined in respect to the agent. For the possessive case before a real participle, denotes not the possessor of something, as in other instances, but the agent of the action, or the subject of the being or passion; and the simple question here is, whether this extraordinary use of the possessive case is, or is not, such an idiom of our language as ought to be justified. Participles may become nouns, if we choose to use them substantively; but can they govern the possessive case before them, while they govern also the objective after them, or while they have a participial meaning which is qualified by adverbs? If they can, Lowth, Murray, and others, are wrong in supposing the foregoing phrases to be ungrammatical, and in teaching that the possessive case before a participle converts it into a noun; and if they cannot, Priestley, Murray, Hiley, Wells, Weld, and others, are wrong in supposing that a participle, or a phrase beginning with a participle, may properly govern the possessive case. Compare Murray's seventh note under his Rule 10th, with the second under his Rule 14th. The same contradiction is taught by many other compilers. See *Smith's New Grammar*, pp. 152 and 162; *Comly's Gram.*, 91 and 108; *Ingersoll's*, 180 and 199.

OBS. 7.—Concerning one of the forms of expression which Murray approves and prefers, among his corrections above, the learned doctors Lowth and Campbell appear to have formed very different opinions. The latter, in the chapter which, in his Philosophy of Rhetoric, he devotes to disputed points in syntax, says: "There is only one other observation of Dr. Lowth, on which, before I conclude this article, I must beg leave to offer some remarks. 'Phrases like the following, though very common, are improper: Much depends upon the *rule's being observed*; and error will be the consequence of *its being neglected*. For here *is* a noun *and* a pronoun representing it, each in the possessive case, that is, under the government of another noun, but without other noun to govern it: for *being observed*, and *being neglected*, are not nouns: nor can you supply the place of the possessive case by the preposition *of* before the noun or pronoun.'[346] For my part," continues Campbell, "notwithstanding what is here very speciously urged, I am not satisfied that there is any fault in the phrases censured. They appear to me to be perfectly in the idiom of our tongue, and such as on some occasions could not easily be avoided, unless by recurring to circumlocution, an expedient which invariably tends to enervate the expression."—*Philosophy of Rhetoric*, B. ii, Ch. iv, p. 234.

OBS. 8.—Dr. Campbell, if I understand his argument, defends the foregoing expressions against the objections of Dr. Lowth, not on the ground that participles as such may govern the possessive case, but on the supposition that as the simple active participle may become a noun, and in that character govern the possessive case, so may the passive participle, and with equal propriety, notwithstanding it consists of two or more words, which must in this construction be considered as forming "one compound noun." I am not sure that he means to confine himself strictly to this latter ground, but if he does, his position cannot be said in any respect to contravene my rule for the possessive case. I do not, however, agree with him, either in the opinion which he offers, or in the negative which he attempts to prove. In view of the two examples, "Much depends upon the *rule's being observed*," and, "Much depends upon *their observing of the rule*," he says: "Now, although I allow both *the* modes of expression to be good, I think the first *simpler and better* than the second." Then, denying all faults, he proceeds: "Let us consider whether the former be liable to *any objections*, which do not equally affect the latter." But in his argument, he considers only the objections offered by Lowth, which indeed he sufficiently refutes. Now to me there appear to be other objections, which are better founded. In the first place, the two sentences are not equivalent in meaning; hence the preference suggested by this critic and others, is absurd. Secondly, a compound noun formed of two or three words without any hyphen, is at best such an anomaly, as we ought rather to avoid than to prefer. If these considerations do not positively condemn the former construction, they ought at least to prevent it from displacing the latter; and seldom is either to be preferred to the regular noun, which we can limit by the article or the possessive at pleasure: as, "Much depends on *an observance* of the rule."—"Much depends on *their observance* of the rule." Now these two sentences are equivalent to the two former, but not to each other; and, *vice versa*: that is, the two former are equivalent to these, but not to each other.[347]

OBS. 9.—From Dr. Campbell's commendation of Lowth, as having "given some excellent directions for preserving a proper distinction between the noun and the gerund,"—that is, between the participial noun and the participle,—it is fair to infer that he meant to preserve it himself; and yet, in the argument above mentioned, he appears to have carelessly framed one ambiguous or very erroneous sentence, from which, as I imagine, his views of this matter have been misconceived, and by which Murray and all his modifiers have been furnished with an example wherewith to confound this distinction, and also to contradict themselves. The sentence is this: "Much will depend on *your pupil's composing*, but more on *his reading* frequently."—*Philos. of Rhet.*, p. 235. Volumes innumerable have gone abroad, into our schools and elsewhere, which pronounce this sentence to be "correct and proper." But after all, what does it mean? Does the adverb "*frequently*" qualify the verb "*will depend*" expressed in the sentence? or "*will depend*" understood after *more*? or both? or neither? Or does this adverb qualify the action of "*reading*?" or the action of "*composing*?" or both? or neither? But *composing* and *reading*, if they are mere *nouns*, cannot properly be qualified by any adverb; and, if they are called participles, the question recurs respecting the possessives. Besides, *composing*, as a participle, is commonly *transitive*; nor is it very fit for a noun, without some adjunct. And, when participles become nouns, their government (it is said) falls upon *of*, and their adverbs are usually converted into adjectives; as, "Much will depend on your *pupil's composing of themes*; but more, on *his frequent reading*." This may not be the author's meaning, for the example was originally composed as a mere mock sentence, or by way of "*experiment*;" and one may doubt whether its meaning was ever at all thought of by the philosopher. But, to make it a respectable example, some correction there must be; for, surely, no man can have any clear idea to communicate, which he cannot better express, than by imitating this loose phraseology. It is scarcely more correct, than to say, "Much will depend on *an author's using*, but more on *his learning* frequently." Yet is it commended as a *model*, either entire or in part, by Murray, Ingersoll, Fisk, R. C. Smith, Cooper, Lennie, Hiley, Bullions, C. Adams, A. H. Weld, and I know not how many other school critics.

OBS. 10.—That singular notion, so common in our grammars, that a participle and its adjuncts may form "*one name*" or "*substantive phrase*," and so govern the possessive case, where it is presumed the participle itself could not, is an invention worthy to have been always ascribed to its true author. For this doctrine, as I suppose, our grammarians are indebted to Dr. Priestley. In his grammar it stands thus: "When an *entire clause* of a sentence, beginning with a participle of the present tense, is used as one name, or to express one idea, or circumstance, the noun on which it depends may be put in the genitive case. Thus, instead of saying, *What is the meaning of this lady holding up her train,* i. e. *what is the meaning of the lady in holding up her train,* we may say, *What is the meaning of this* lady's *holding up her train*; just as we say, *What is the meaning of this lady's dress,* &c. So we may either say, *I remember* it being *reckoned a great exploit;* or, perhaps more elegantly, *I remember* its being *reckoned,* &c."—*Priestley's Gram.,* p. 69. Now, to say nothing of errors in punctuation, capitals, &c., there is scarcely any thing in all this passage, that is either conceived or worded properly. Yet, coining from a Doctor of Laws, and Fellow of the Royal Society, it is readily adopted by Murray, and for his sake by others; and so, with all its blunders, the vain gloss passes uncensured into the schools, as a rule and model for elegant composition. Dr. Priestley pretends to appreciate the difference between participles and participial nouns, but he rather contrives a fanciful distinction in the sense, than a real one in the construction. His only note on this point,—a note about the "*horse running to-day,*" and the "*horse's running* to-day,"—I shall leave till we come to the syntax of participles.

OBS. 11.—Having prepared the reader to understand the origin of what is to follow, I now cite from L. Murray's code a paragraph which appears to be contradictory to his own doctrine, as suggested in the fifth observation above; and not only so, it is irreconcilable with any proper distinction between the participle and the participial noun. "When an *entire clause* of a sentence, beginning with a participle of the present tense, is used as *one name,* or to express one idea or circumstance, the *noun on which it depends* may be put in the *genitive* case; thus, *instead* of saying, 'What is the reason of this *person dismissing* his servant so hastily?' *that is,* 'What is the reason of this person, *in* dismissing his servant so hastily?' we *may* say, and *perhaps* ought to say, 'What is the reason of this *person's* dismissing of his servant *so hastily?*' Just as we say, 'What is the reason of this person's *hasty dismission* of his servant?' So also, we say, 'I remember it being reckoned a great exploit;' or more properly, 'I remember *its* being reckoned,' &c. The following sentence is *correct and proper*: 'Much will depend on *the pupil's composing*, but more on *his reading* frequently.' It would not be accurate to say, 'Much will depend on the *pupil composing*.' &c. We also properly say; 'This will be the effect *of the pupil's composing* frequently;' instead of, '*Of the pupil composing* frequently.' The *participle*, in such constructions, *does the office* of a substantive; and it should therefore have a CORRESPONDENT REGIMEN."—*Murray's Gram.*, Rule 10th, Note 7; *Ingersoll's*, p. 180; *Fisk's*, 108; *R. C. Smith's*, 152; *Alger's*, 61; *Merchant's*, 84. See also *Weld's Gram.*, 2d Ed., p. 150; "Abridged Ed.," 117.[348]

OBS. 12.—Now, if it were as easy to prove that a participle, as such, or (what amounts to the same thing) a phrase beginning with a participle, ought never to govern the possessive case, as it is to show that every part and parcel of the foregoing citations from Priestley, Murray, and others, is both weakly conceived and badly written, I should neither have detained the reader so long on this topic, nor ever have placed it among the most puzzling points of grammar. Let it be observed, that what these writers absurdly call "*an entire* CLAUSE *of a sentence*," is found on examination to be some *short* PHRASE, the participle with its adjuncts, or even the participle alone, or with a single adverb only; as, "holding up her train,"—"dismissing his servant so hastily,"—"composing,"—"reading frequently,"—"composing frequently." And each of these, with an opposite error as great, they will have to be "*one name*," and to convey but "*one idea*;" supposing that by virtue of this imaginary oneness, it may govern the possessive case, and signify something which a "lady," or a "person," or a "pupil," may consistently *possess*. And then, to be wrong in every thing, they suggest that any noun on which such a participle, with its adjuncts, "depends, *may be put* in the *genitive case*;" whereas, such a change is seldom, if ever, admissible, and in our language, no participle *ever can depend* on any other than the nominative or the objective case. Every participle so depending is an adjunct to the noun; and every possessive, in its turn, is an adjunct to the word which governs it. In respect to construction, no terms differ more than a participle which governs the possessive case, and a participle which does not. These different constructions the contrivers of the foregoing rule, here take to be equivalent in meaning; whereas they elsewhere pretend to find in them quite different significations. The meaning is sometimes very different, and sometimes very similar; but seldom, if ever, are the terms convertible. And even if they were so, and the difference were nothing, would it not be better to adhere, where we can, to the analogy of General Grammar? In Greek and Latin, a participle may agree with a noun in the genitive case; but, if we regard analogy, that genitive must be Englished, not by the possessive case, but by *of* and the objective; as, "[Greek: 'Epeì dokim`æn zæteîte toû 'en 'emoì laloûntos Christoû.]"—"Quandoquidem experimentum quæritis in me loquentis Christi."—*Beza.* "Since ye seek a proof of *Christ speaking* in me."—*2 Cor.*, xiii, 3. We might here, perhaps, say, "of *Christ's speaking* in me," but is not the other form better? The French version is, "Puisque vous cherchez une preuve *que Christ parle* par moi;" and this, too, might be imitated in English: "Since ye seek a proof *that Christ speaks* by me."

OBS. 13.—As prepositions very naturally govern any of our participles except the simple perfect, it undoubtedly seems agreeable to our idiom not to disturb this government, when we would express the subject or agent of the being, action, or passion, between the preposition and the participle. Hence we find that the doer or the sufferer of the action is usually made its possessor, whenever the sense does not positively demand a different reading. Against this construction there is seldom any objection, if the participle be taken entirely as a noun, so that it may be called a participial noun; as, "Much depends *on their observing of* the rule."—*Lowth, Campbell*, and *L. Murray*. On the other hand, the participle after the objective is unobjectionable, if the noun or pronoun be the leading word in sense; as, "It would be idle to profess an apprehension of serious *evil resulting* in any respect from the utmost *publicity being given* to its contents."—*London Eclectic Review,* 1816. "The following is a beautiful instance of the *sound* of words *corresponding* to motion."—*Murray's Gram.*, i, p. 333. "We shall discover many *things partaking* of both those characters."—*West's Letters*, p. 182. "To a *person following* the vulgar mode of omitting the comma."—*Churchill's Gram.*, p. 365. But, in comparing the different constructions above noticed, writers are frequently puzzled to determine, and frequently too do they err in determining, which word shall be made the adjunct, and which the leading term. Now, wherever there is much doubt which of the two forms ought to be preferred, I think we may well conclude that both are wrong; especially, if there can easily be found for the idea an other expression that is undoubtedly clear and correct. Examples: "These appear to be instances of the present *participle being used* passively."—*Murray's Gram.*, p. 64. "These are examples of the past *participle being applied* in an active sense."—*Ib.*, 64. "We have some examples of *adverbs being used* for substantives."—*Priestley's Gram.*, p. 134; *Murray's*, 198; *Ingersoll's*, 206; *Fisk's*, 140; *Smith's*, 165. "By a *noun, pronoun,* or *adjective, being prefixed* to the substantive."—*Murray's Gram.*, p. 39; also *Ingersoll's, Fisk's, Alger's, Maltby's, Merchant's, Bacon's,* and others. Here, if their own rule is good for any thing, these authors ought rather to have preferred the possessive case; but strike out the word *being*, which is not necessary to the sense, and all question about the construction vanishes. Or if any body will justify these examples as they stand, let him observe that there are others, without number, to be justified on the same principle; as, "Much depends *on the rule being observed.*"—"Much will depend *on the pupil composing frequently.*" Again: "Cyrus did not wait for the *Babylonians coming* to attack him."—*Rollin*, ii, 86. "Cyrus did not wait for the *Babylonians' coming* to attack him." That is—"for *their* coming," and not, "for *them* coming;" but much better than either: "Cyrus did not wait for the Babylonians *to come and* attack him." Again: "To prevent his *army's being* enclosed and hemmed in."—*Rollin*, ii, 89. "To prevent his *army being* enclosed and hemmed in." Both are wrong. Say, "To prevent his *army from being* enclosed and hemmed in." Again: "As a sign of *God's fulfilling* the promise."—*Rollin*, ii, 23. "As a sign of *God fulfilling* the promise." Both are objectionable. Say, "As a sign *that God would fulfill* the promise." Again: "There is affirmative evidence for *Moses's being* the author of these books."—*Bp. Watson's Apology*, p. 28. "The first argument you produce against *Moses being* the author of these books."—*Ib.*, p. 29.

Both are bad. Say,—"for *Moses as being* the author,"—"against *Moses as being* the author," &c.

OBS. 14.—Now, although thousands of sentences might easily be quoted, in which the possessive case is *actually* governed by a participle, and that participle not taken in every respect as a noun; yet I imagine, there are, of this kind, few examples, if any, the meaning of which might not be *better expressed* in some other way. There are surely none among all the examples which are presented by Priestley, Murray, and others, under their rule above. Nor would a thousand such as are there given, amount to any proof of the rule. They are all of them *unreal* or *feigned* sentences, made up for the occasion, and, like most others that are produced in the same way, made up badly—made up after some ungrammatical model. If a gentleman could possibly demand a *lady's meaning* in such an act as *the holding-up of her train*, he certainly would use none of Priestley's three questions, which, with such ridiculous and uninstructive pedantry, are repeated and expounded by Latham, in his Hand-Book, §481; but would probably say, "Madam, *what do you mean* by holding up your train?" It was folly for the doctor to ask *an other person*, as if an other could *guess* her meaning better than he. The text with the possessive is therefore not to be corrected by inserting a hyphen and an *of*, after Murray's doctrine before cited; as, "What is the meaning of this *lady's holding-up of* her train?" Murray did well to reject this example, but as a specimen of English, his own is no better. The question which he asks, ought to have been, "*Why did this person dismiss* his servant so hastily?" Fisk has it in the following form: "What is the reason of this *person's dismissing his servant* so hastily?"—*English Grammar Simplified*, p. 108. This amender of grammars omits the *of* which Murray and others scrupulously insert to govern the noun *servant*, and boldly avows at once, what their rule implies, that, "Participles are sometimes used both as verbs and as nouns at the same time; as, 'By the *mind's changing the object*,' &c."—*Ib.*, p. 134; so *Emmons's Gram.*, p. 64.

But he errs as much as they, and contradicts both himself and them. For one ought rather to say, "By the *mind's changing of* the object;" else *changing,* which "does the office of a noun," has not truly "a correspondent regimen." Yet *of* is useless after *dismissing,* unless we take away the *adverb* by which the participle is prevented from becoming a noun. "Dismissing *of* his servant so *hastily,*" is in itself an ungrammatical phrase; and nothing but to omit either the preposition, or the two adverbs, can possibly make it right. Without the latter, it may follow the possessive; but without the former, our most approved grammars say it cannot. Some critics, however, object to the *of,* because *the dismissing* is not *the servant's* act; but this, as I shall hereafter show, is no valid objection: they stickle for a false rule.

OBS. 15.—Thus these authors, differing from one an other as they do, and each contradicting himself and some of the rest, are, as it would seem, all wrong in respect to the whole matter at issue. For whether the phrase in question be like Priestley's, or like Murray's, or like Fisk's, it is still, according to the best authorities, unfit to govern the possessive case; because, in stead of being a substantive, it is something more than a participle, and yet they take it substantively. They form this phrase in many different fashions, and yet each man of them pretends that what he approves, is just like the construction of a regular noun: "*Just as we say,* 'What is the reason of this person's *hasty dismission of* his servant.'"—*Murray, Fisk, and others.* "*Just as we say,* 'What is the meaning of this lady's *dress,*' &c."—*Priestley.* The meaning of a *lady's dress,* forsooth! The illustration is worthy of the doctrine taught. "*An entire clause of a sentence*" substantively possessed, is sufficiently like "*the meaning of a lady's dress, &c.*" Cobbett despised *andsoforths,* for their lack of meaning; and I find none in this one, unless it be, "*of tinsel and of fustian.*" This gloss therefore I wholly disapprove, judging the position more tenable, to deny, if we consequently must, that either a phrase or a participle, as such, can consistently govern the possessive case. For whatever word or term gives rise to the direct relation of property, and is rightly made to govern the possessive case, ought in reason to be a *noun*—ought to be the name of some substance, quality, state, action, passion, being, or thing. When therefore other parts of speech assume this relation, they naturally *become nouns*; as, "Against the day of *my burying*."—*John*, xii, 7. "Till the day of *his showing* unto Israel."—*Luke*, i, 80. "By *my own showing*."—*Cowper, Life*, p. 22. "By a fortune of *my own getting*."—*Ib.* "Let *your yea* be yea, and *your nay* nay."—*James*, v, 12. "Prate of *my whereabout*."—*Shah.*

OBS. 16.—The government of possessives by "*entire clauses*" or "*substantive phrases*," as they are sometimes called, I am persuaded, may best be disposed of, in almost every instance, by charging the construction with impropriety or awkwardness, and substituting for it some better phraseology. For example, our grammars abound with sentences like the following, and call them good English: (1.) "So we may either say, 'I remember *it being* reckoned a great exploit;' or perhaps more elegantly, 'I remember *its being* reckoned a great exploit.'"—*Priestley, Murray, and others*. Here both modes are wrong; the latter, especially; because it violates a general rule of syntax, in regard to the case of the noun *exploit*. Say, "I remember *it* was reckoned a great exploit." Again: (2.) "We also properly say, 'This will be the effect of the *pupil's composing* frequently.'"—*Murray's Gram.*, p. 179; *and others*. Better, "This will be the effect, *if the pupil compose* frequently." But this sentence is *fictitious*, and one may doubt whether good authors can be found who use *compose* or *composing* as being intransitive. (3.) "What can be the reason of the *committee's having delayed* this business?"—*Murray's Key*, p. 223. Say, "*Why have the committee* delayed this business?" (4.) "What can be the cause of the *parliament's neglecting* so important a business?"—*Ib.*, p. 195. Say, "*Why does the parliament neglect* so important a business?" (5.) "The time of *William's making* the experiment, at length arrived."—*Ib.*, p. 195. Say, "The time *for William to make* the experiment, at length arrived." (6.) "I hope this is the last time of *my acting* so imprudently."—*Ib.*, p. 263. Say, "I hope *I shall never again act* so imprudently." (7.) "If I were to give a reason for *their looking so well*, it would be, that they rise early."—*Ib.*, p. 263. Say, "I should attribute *their healthful appearance* to their early rising." (8.) "The tutor said, that diligence and application to study were necessary to *our becoming* good scholars."—*Cooper's Gram.*, p. 145. Here is an anomaly in the construction of the noun *scholars*. Say, "The tutor said, that *diligent application* to study was necessary to our *success in learning.*" (9.) "The reason of *his having acted* in the manner he did, was not fully explained."—*Murray's Key*, p. 263. This author has a very singular mode of giving "STRENGTH" to weak sentences. The faulty text here was. "The reason why he *acted* in the manner he did, was not fully explained."—*Murray's Exercises*, p. 131. This is much better than the other, but I should choose to say. "The reason of *his conduct* was not fully explained." For, surely, the "one idea or circumstance" of his "having acted in the manner in *which* he did act," may be quite as forcibly named by the one word *conduct,* as by all this verbiage, this "substantive phrase," or "entire clause," of such cumbrous length.

OBS. 17.—The foregoing observations tend to show, that the government of possessives by participles, is in general a construction little to be commended, if at all allowed. I thus narrow down the application of the principle, but do not hereby determine it to be altogether wrong. There are other arguments, both for and against the doctrine, which must be taken into the account, before we can fully decide the question. The double construction which may be given to infinitive verbs; the Greek idiom which allows to such verbs an article before them and an objective after them; the mixed character of the Latin gerund, part noun, part verb; the use or substitution of the participle in English for the gerund in Latin;—all these afford so many reasons by analogy, for allowing that our participle—except it be the perfect—since it participates the properties of a verb and a noun, as well as those of a verb and an adjective, may unite in itself a double construction, and be taken substantively in one relation, and participially in an other. Accordingly some grammarians so define it; and many writers so use it; both parties disregarding the distinction between the participle and the participial noun, and justifying the construction of the former, not only as a proper participle after its noun, and as a gerundive after its preposition; not only as a participial adjective before its noun, and as a participial noun, in the regular syntax of a noun; but also as a mixed term, in the double character of noun and participle at once. Nor are these its only uses; for, after an auxiliary, it is the main verb; and in a few instances, it passes into a preposition, an adverb, or something else. Thus have we from the verb a single derivative, which fairly ranks with about half the different parts of speech, and takes distinct constructions even more numerous; and yet these authors scruple not to make of it a hybridous thing, neither participle nor noun, but constructively both. "But this," says Lowth, "is inconsistent; let it be either the one or the other, and abide by its proper construction."—*Gram.*, p. 82. And so say I—as asserting the general principle, and leaving the reader to judge of its exceptions. Because, without this mongrel character, the participle in our language has a multiplicity of uses unparalleled in any other; and because it seldom happens that the idea intended by this double construction may not be otherwise expressed more elegantly. But if it sometimes seem proper that the gerundive participle should be allowed to govern the possessive case, no exception to my rule is needed for the *parsing* of such possessive; because whatever is invested with such government, whether rightly or wrongly, is assumed as "the name of something possessed."

OBS. 18.—The reader may have observed, that in the use of participial nouns, the distinction of *voice* in the participle is sometimes disregarded. Thus, "Against the day of my *burying*," means, "Against the day of my *being buried*." But in this instance the usual noun *burial* or *funeral* would have been better than either: "Against the day of *my burial*." I. e., "In diem *funerationis meæ*."—*Beza*. "In diem *sepulturæ meæ*."—*Leusden*. "[Greek: 'Eis t`æn hæméran toû entaphiasmoû mou.]"—*John*, xii, 7. In an other text, this noun is very properly used for the Greek infinitive, and the Latin gerund; as, "*For my burial*."—*Matt*., xxvi, 12. "Ad *funerandum* me."—*Beza*. "Ad *sepeliendum* me."—*Leusden*. Literally: "*For burying me*." "[Greek: Pròs tò entaphiásai me.]" Nearly: "*For to have me buried*." Not all that is allowable, is commendable; and if either of the uncompounded terms be found a fit substitute for the compound participial noun, it is better to dispense with the latter, on account of its dissimilarity to other nouns: as, "Which only proceed upon the *question's being begged*."—*Barclay's Works*, Vol. iii, p. 361. Better, "Which only proceed upon *a begging of the question*." "The *king's having conquered* in the battle, established his throne."—*Nixon's Parser*, p. 128. Better, "The king's *conquering* in the battle;" for, in the participial noun, the distinction of *tense*, or of previous *completion*, is as needless as that of voice. "The *fleet's having sailed* prevented mutiny."—*Ib*., p. 78. Better, "The *sailing of the fleet*,"—or, "The *fleet's sailing*" &c. "The *prince's being murdered* excited their pity."—*Ibid*. Better, "The *prince's murder* excited their *indignation*."

OBS. 19.—In some instances, as it appears, not a little difficulty is experienced by our grammarians, respecting the addition or the omission of the possessive sign, the terminational apostrophic *s*, which in nouns is the ordinary index of the possessive case. Let it be remembered that every possessive is governed, or ought to be governed, by some noun expressed or understood, except such as (without the possessive sign) are put in apposition with others so governed; and for every possessive termination there must be a separate governing word, which, if it is not expressed, is shown by the possessive sign to be understood. The possessive sign itself *may* and *must* be omitted in certain cases; but, because it can never be inserted or discarded without suggesting or discarding a governing noun, it is never omitted *by ellipsis*, as Buchanan, Murray, Nixon, and many others, erroneously teach. The four lines of Note 2d below, are sufficient to show, in every instance, when it must be used, and when omitted; but Murray, after as many octavo pages on the point, still leaves it perplexed and undetermined. If a person knows what he means to say, let him express it according to the Note, and he will not fail to use just as many apostrophes and Esses as he ought. How absurd then is that common doctrine of ignorance, which Nixon has gathered from Allen and Murray, his chief oracles! "If *several* nouns in the *genitive* case, are immediately connected by a *conjunction*, the apostrophic *s* is annexed *to the last*, but *understood to the rest*; as, Neither *John* (i. e. John's) nor *Eliza's* books."—*English Parser*, p. 115. The author gives fifteen other examples like this, all of them bad English, or at any rate, not adapted to the sense which he intends!

OBS. 20.—The possessive case generally comes *immediately before* the governing noun, expressed or understood; as, "All *nature's* difference keeps all *nature's* peace."—*Pope*. "Lady! be *thine* (i. e., *thy walk*) the *Christian's* walk."—*Chr. Observer.* "Some of *Æschylus's* [plays] and *Euripides's* plays are opened in this manner."—*Blair's Rhet.*, p. 459. And in this order one possessive sometimes governs an other: as, "*Peter's wife's mother*;"—"*Paul's sister's son.*"—*Bible*. But, to this general principle of arrangement, there are some exceptions: as,

1. When the governing noun has an adjective, this may intervene; as, "*Flora's* earliest *smells*."—*Milton*. "Of *man's* first disobedience."—*Id.* In the following phrase from the Spectator, "Of *Will's* last *night's* lecture," it is not very clear, whether *Will's* is governed by *night's* or by *lecture*; yet it violates a general principle of our grammar, to suppose the latter; because, on this supposition, two possessives, each having the sign, will be governed by one noun.

2. When the possessive is affirmed or denied; as, "The book is *mine*, and not *John's*." But here the governing noun *may be supplied* in its proper place; and, in some such instances, it *must* be, else a pronoun or the verb will be the only governing word: as, "Ye are *Christ's* [disciples, or people]; and Christ is *God's*" [son].—*St. Paul*. Whether this phraseology is thus elliptical or not, is questionable. See Obs. 4th, in this series.

3. When the case occurs without the sign, either by apposition or by connexion; as, "In her *brother Absalom's* house."—*Bible*. "*David* and *Jonathan's* friendship."—*Allen*. "*Adam* and *Eve's* morning hymn."—*Dr. Ash*. "Behold the heaven, and the heaven of heavens, is the *Lord's* thy God."—*Deut.,*, x, 14. "For *peace* and *quiet's* sake."—*Cowper*. "To the beginning of *King James* the *First's* reign."—*Bolingbroke, on Hist.*, p. 32.

OBS. 21—The possessive case is in general (though not always) equivalent to the preposition *of* and *the objective*; as, "*Of* Judas Iscariot, *Simon's* son."—*John*, xiii, 2. "*To* Judas Iscariot, the son *of Simon*."—*Ib.*, xiii, 26. On account of this one-sided equivalence, many grammarians erroneously reckon the latter to be a "*genitive case*" as well as the former. But they ought to remember, that the preposition is used more frequently than the possessive, and in a variety of senses that cannot be interpreted by this case; as, "*Of* some *of* the books *of* each *of* these classes *of* literature, a catalogue will be given at the end *of* the work."—*L. Murray's Gram.*, p. 178. Murray calls this a "laborious mode of expression," and doubtless it might be a little improved by substituting *in* for the third *of*; but my argument is, that the meaning conveyed cannot be expressed by possessives. The notion that *of* forms a genitive case, led Priestley to suggest, that our language admits a "*double genitive*;" as, "This book *of* my friend's."—*Priestley's Gram.*, p. 71. "It is a discovery *of* Sir Isaac Newton's."—*Ib.*, p. 72. "This exactness *of his*."—STERNE: *ib*. The doctrine has since passed into nearly all our grammars; yet is there no double case here, as I shall presently show.

OBS. 22.—Where the governing noun cannot be easily mistaken, it is often omitted by ellipsis: as, "At the alderman's" [*house*];—"St. Paul's" [*church*];—"A book of my brother's" [*books*];—"A subject of the emperor's" [*subjects*];—"A friend of mine;" i. e., *one of my friends*. "Shall we say that Sacrificing was a pure invention of *Adam's*, or of *Cain* or *Abel's*?"—*Leslie, on Tythes*, p. 93. That is—of Adam's *inventions*, or of Cain or Abel's *inventions*. The Rev. David Blair, unable to resolve this phraseology to his own satisfaction, absurdly sets it down among what he calls "ERRONEOUS OR VULGAR PHRASES." His examples are these: "A poem of Pope's;"—"A soldier of the king's;"—"That is a horse of my father's."—*Blair's Practical Gram.*, p. 110, 111. He ought to have supplied the plural nouns, *poems, soldiers, horses*. This is the true explanation of all the "double genitives" which our grammarians discover; for when the first noun is *partitive*, it naturally suggests more or other things of the same kind, belonging to this possessor; and when such is not the meaning, this construction is improper. In the following example, the noun *eyes* is understood after *his*:

"Ev'n *his*, the *warrior's eyes*, were forced to yield,
That saw, without a tear, Pharsalia's field."
—*Rowe's Lucan*, B. viii, l. 144.

OBS. 23.—When two or more nouns of the possessive form are in any way connected, they usually refer to things individually different but of the same name; and when such is the meaning, the governing noun, which we always suppress somewhere to avoid tautology, is *understood* wherever the sign is added without it; as, "A *father's* or *mother's sister* is an aunt."—*Dr. Webster*. That is, "A *father's sister* or a mother's sister is an aunt." "In the same commemorative acts of the senate, *were thy name*, thy *father's*, thy *brother's*, and the *emperor's*."—*Zenobia*, Vol. i, p. 231.

"From Stiles's pocket into *Nokes's*" [pocket].
—*Hudibras*, B. iii, C. iii, l. 715.

"Add *Nature's, Custom's, Reason's,* Passion's strife."
—*Pope, Brit. Poets*, Vol. vi, p. 383.

It will be observed that in all these examples the governing noun is singular; and, certainly, it must be so, if, with more than one possessive sign, we mean to represent each possessor as having or possessing but one object. If the noun be made plural where it is expressed, it will also be plural where it is implied. It is good English to say, "A *father's* or *mother's sisters* are aunts;" but the meaning is, "A father's *sisters* or a mother's sisters are aunts." But a recent school critic teaches differently, thus: "When different things of the same name belong to different possessors, the sign should be annexed to each; as, *Adams's, Davies's,* and *Perkins'* Arithmetics; i. e., *three different books*."—*Spencer's Gram.*, p. 47. Here the example is fictitious, and has almost as many errors as words. It would be much better English to say, "*Adams's, Davies's, and Perkins's Arithmetic*;" though the objective form with *of* would, perhaps, be still more agreeable for these peculiar names. Spencer, whose Grammar abounds with useless repetitions, repeats his note elsewhere, with the following illustrations: "E. g. *Olmstead's* and *Comstock's* Philosophies. *Gould's Adam's* Latin Grammar."—*Ib.*, p. 106. The latter example is no better suited to his text, than "*Peter's wife's mother*;" and the former is fit only to mean, "Olmstead's *Philosophies* and Comstock's Philosophies." To speak of the two books only, say," Olmstead's *Philosophy* and Comstock's."

www.ingramcontent.com/pod-product-compliance
Lightning Source LLC
Chambersburg PA
CBHW081618100526
44590CB00021B/3496